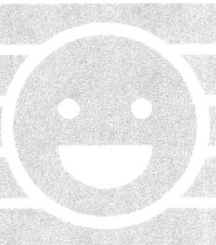

DRAW
~~DRIVE~~ **FAST**
DON'T STOP

SPECIAL ISSUE
SKETCHBOOKS

SKETCH

SKETCH

SKETCH

SKETCH

SKETCH

SKETCH

BOOKS

BOOKS

BOOKS

BOOKS

BOOKS

BOOKS

DOODLE

DOODLE

DOODLE

DOODLE

DOODLE

DOODLE

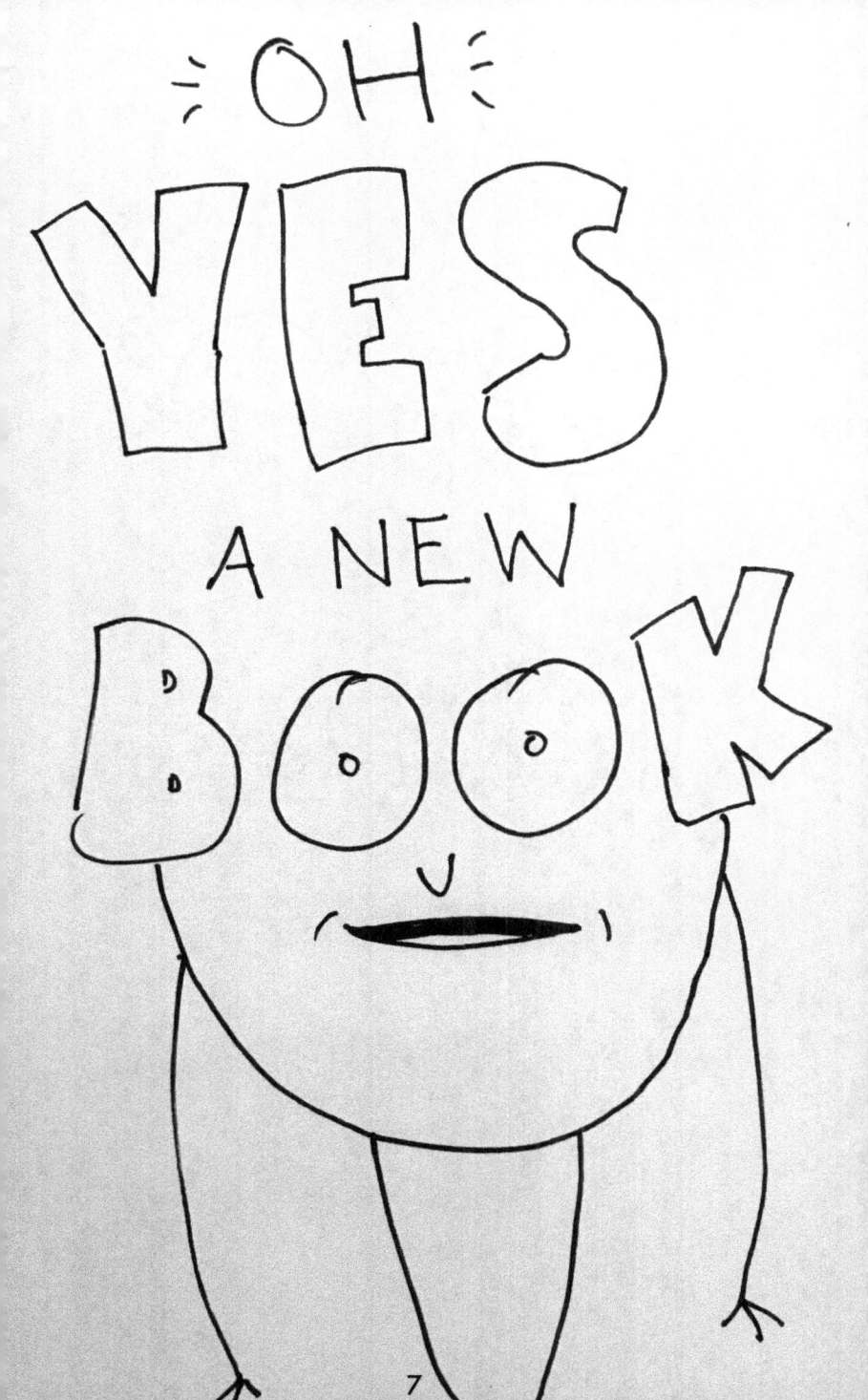

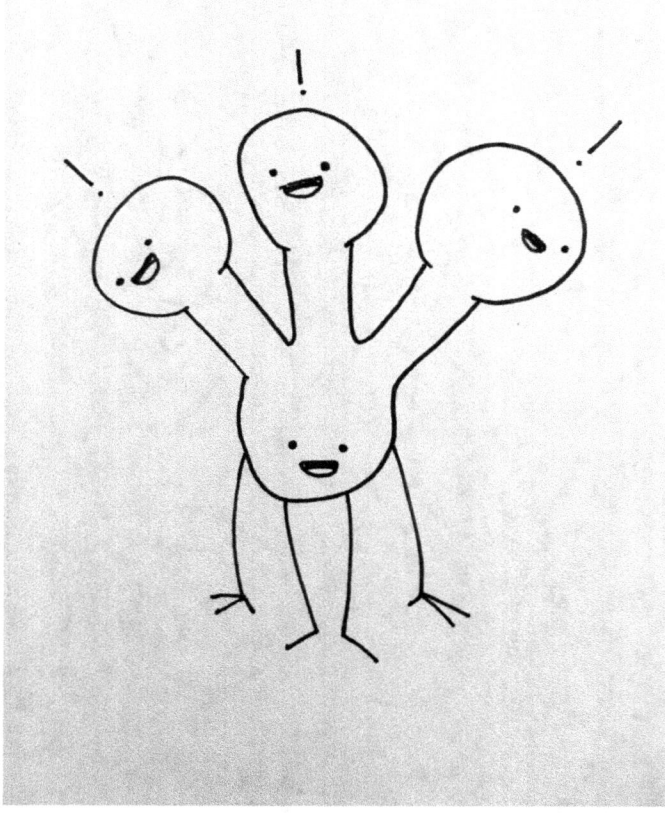

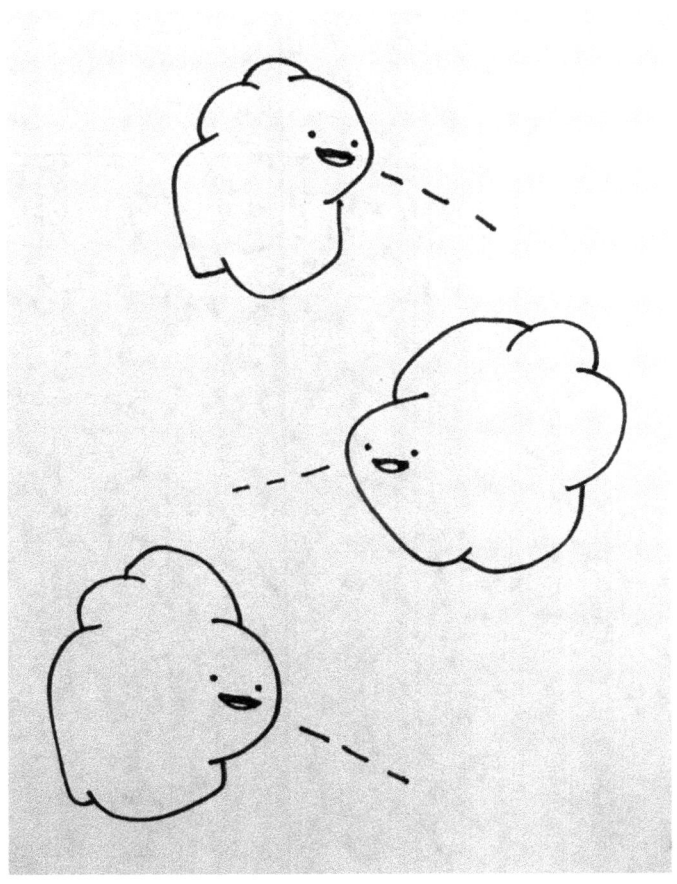

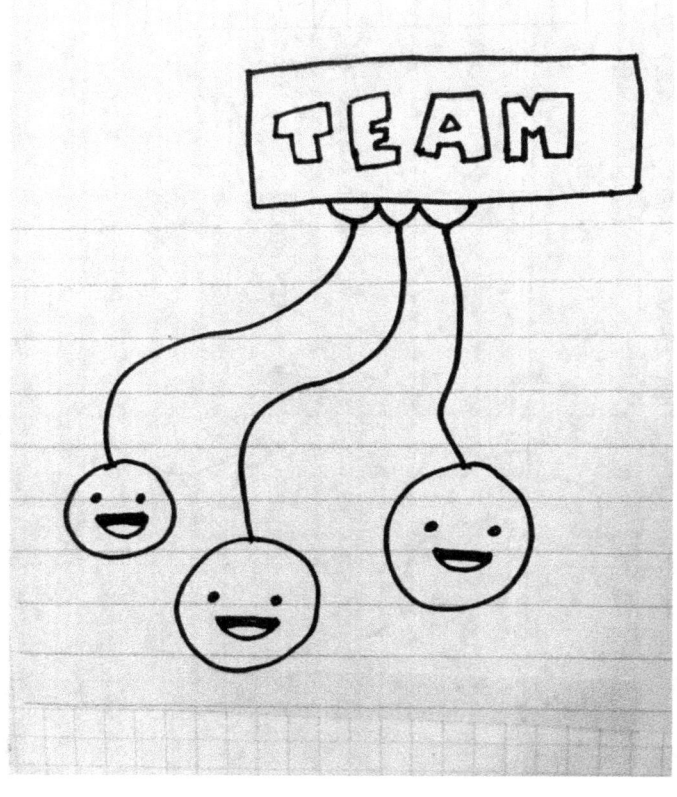

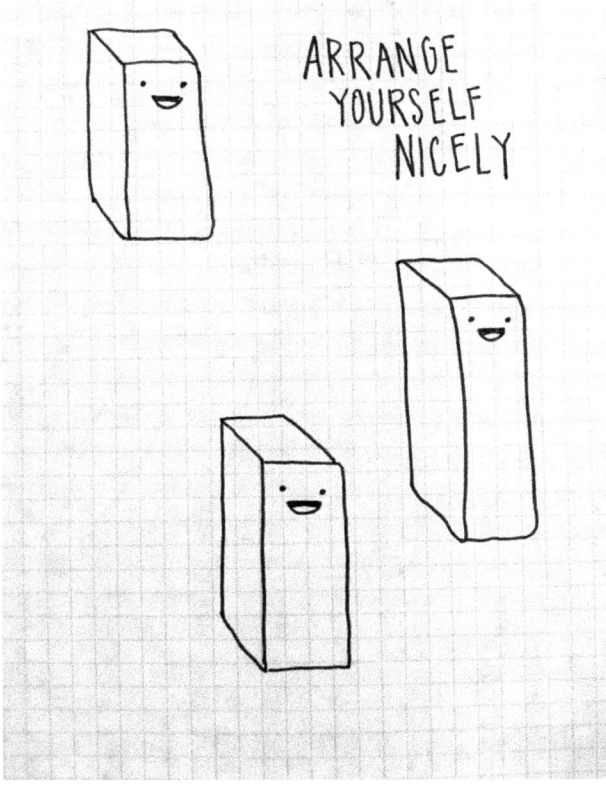

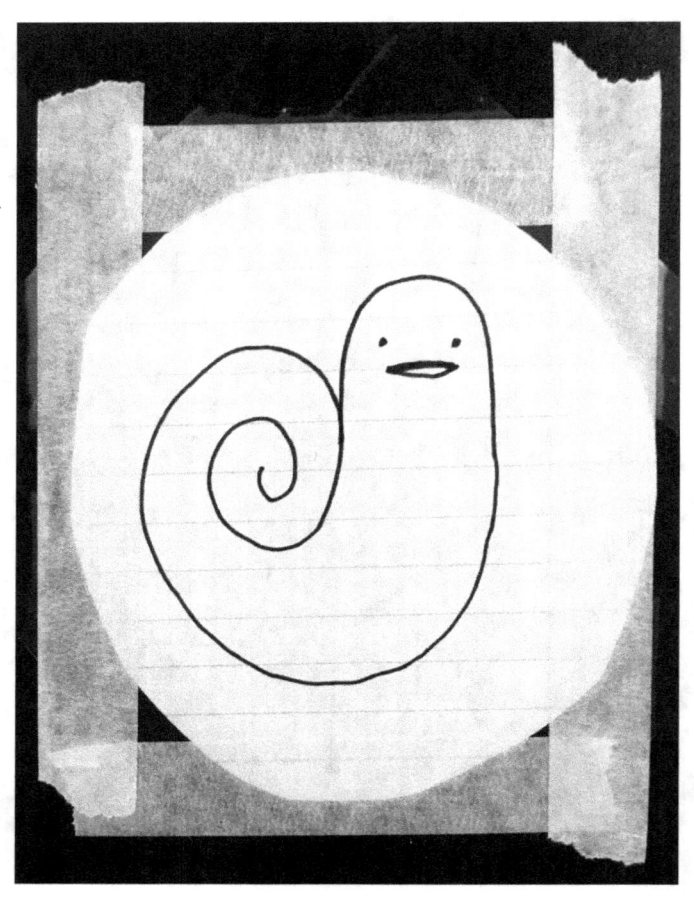

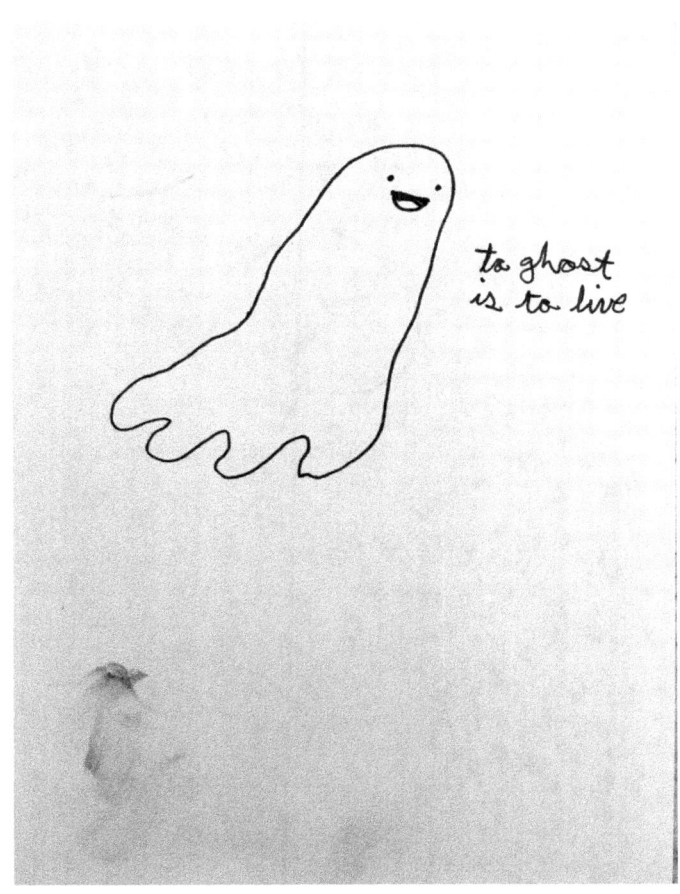

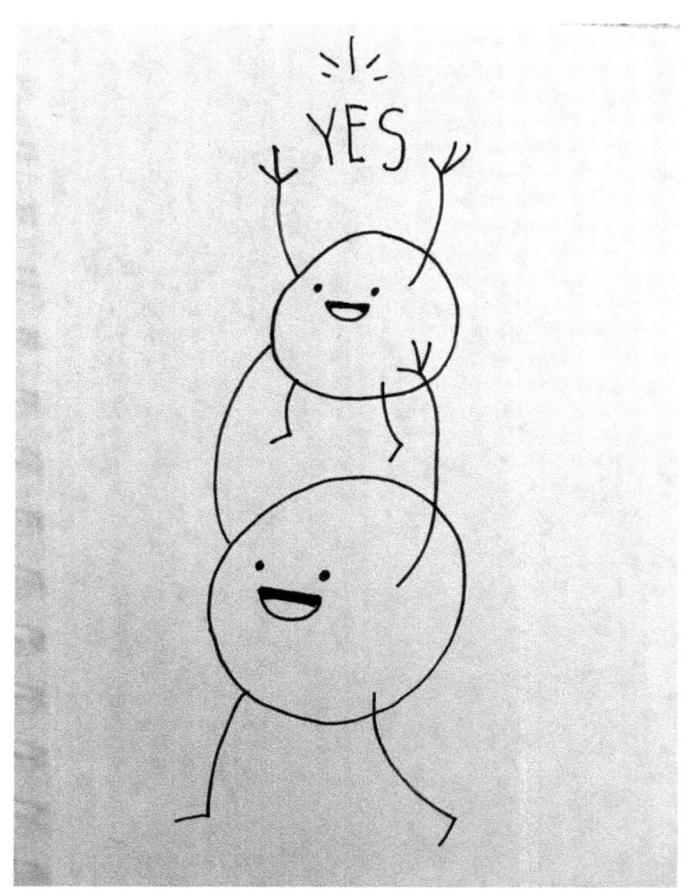

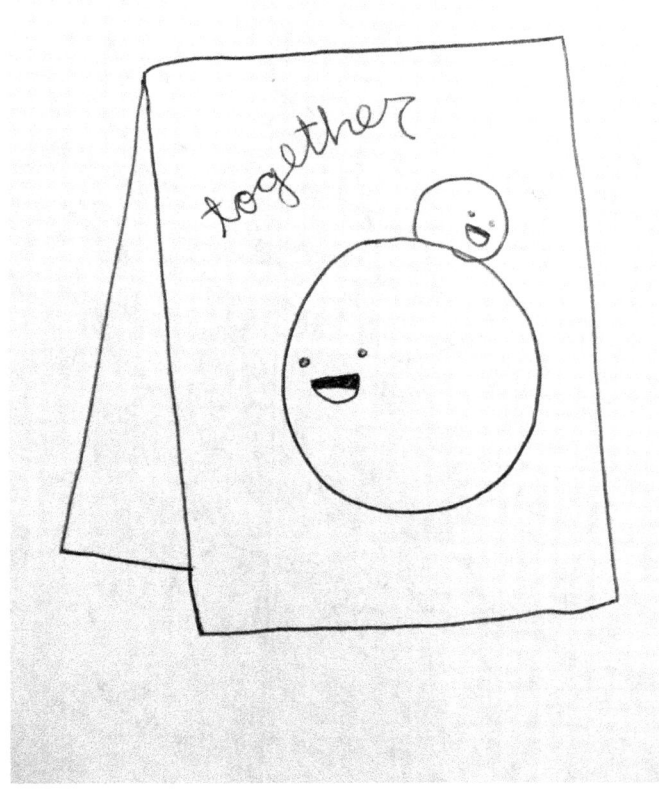

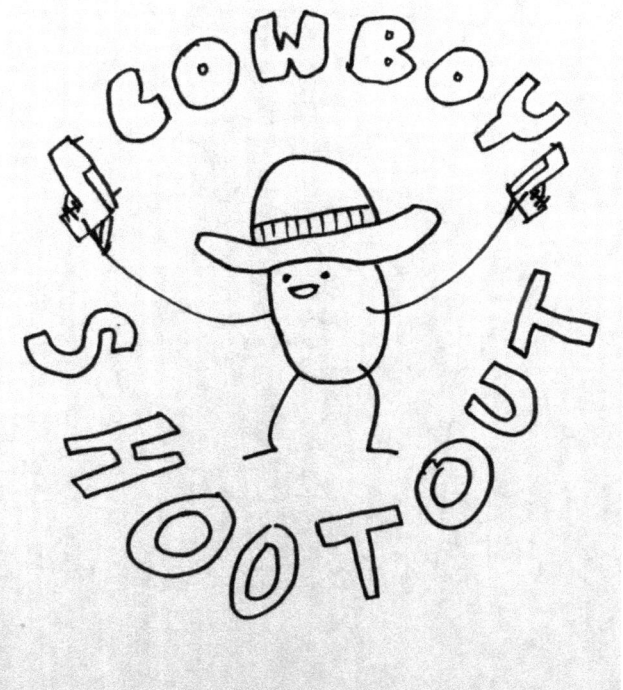

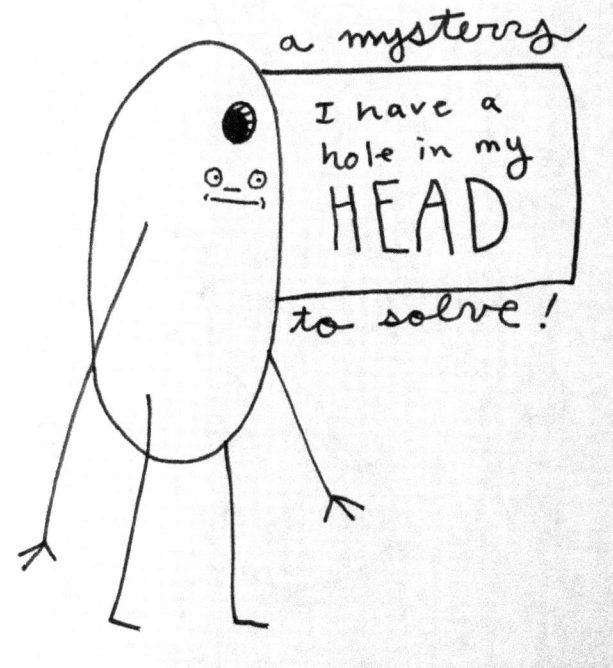

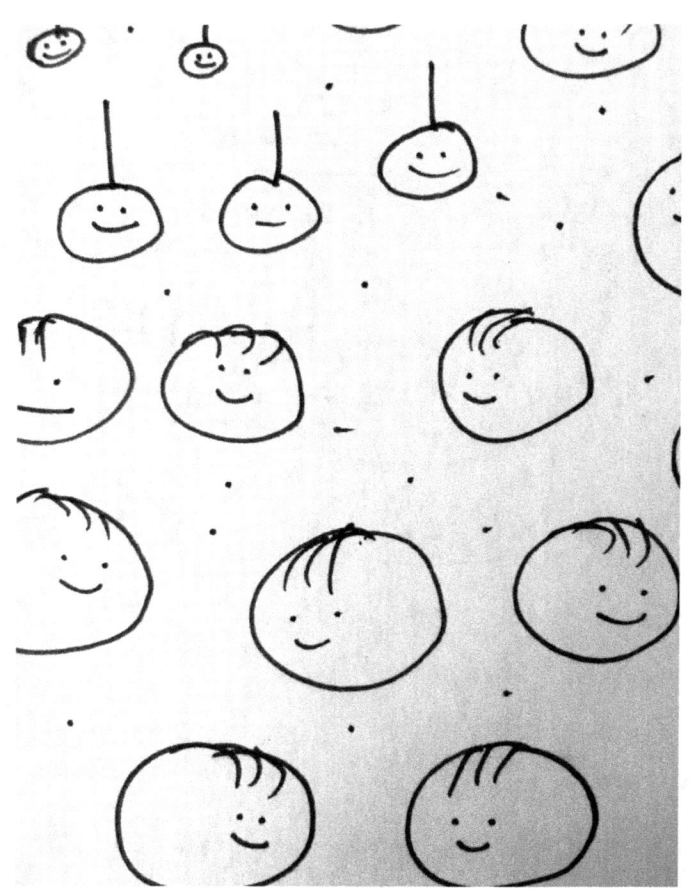

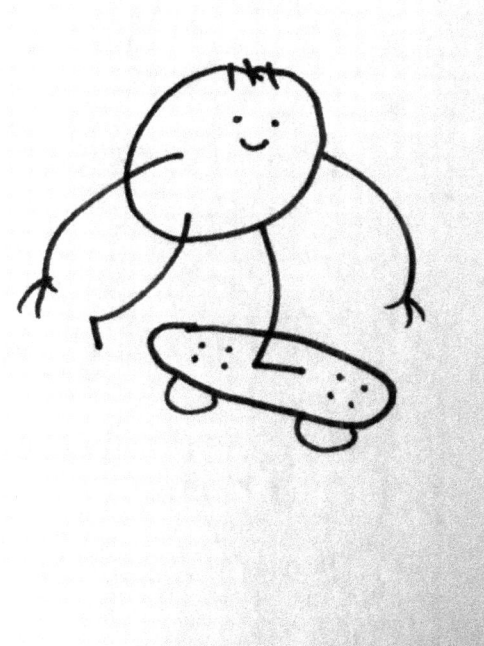

Sorry.

No can do.

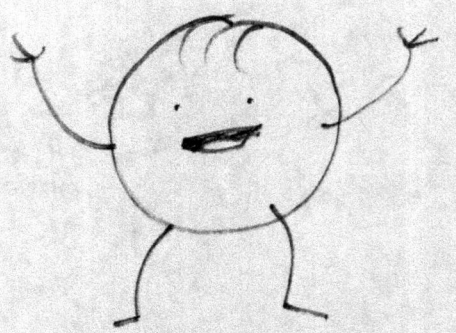

LOSER
patrol
ON
duty

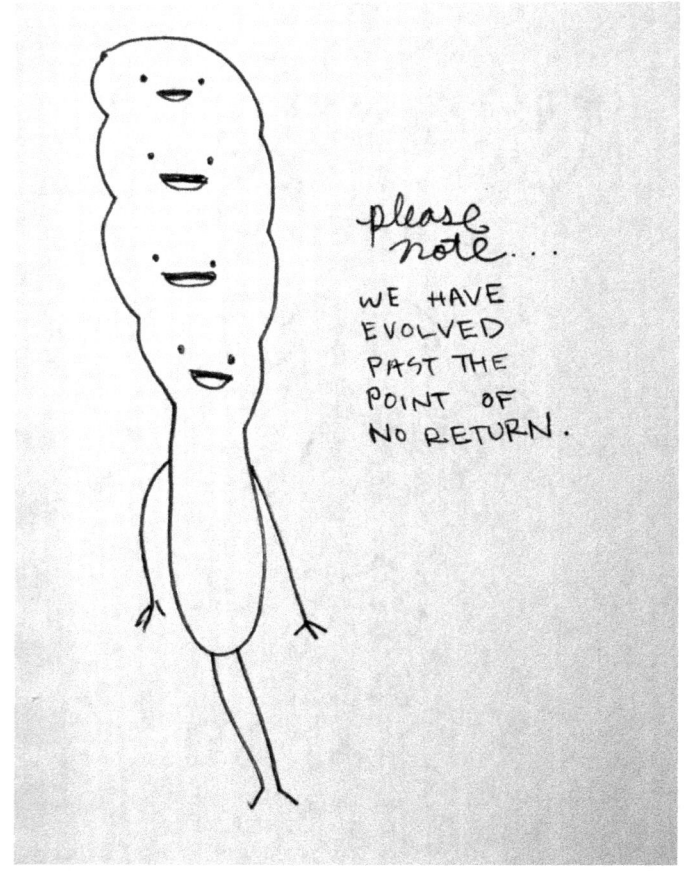

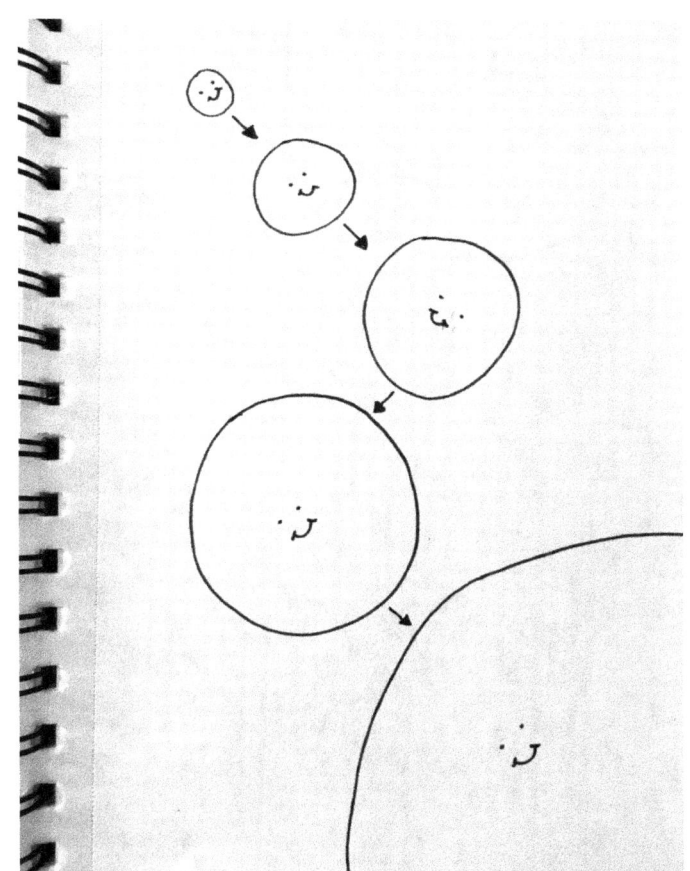

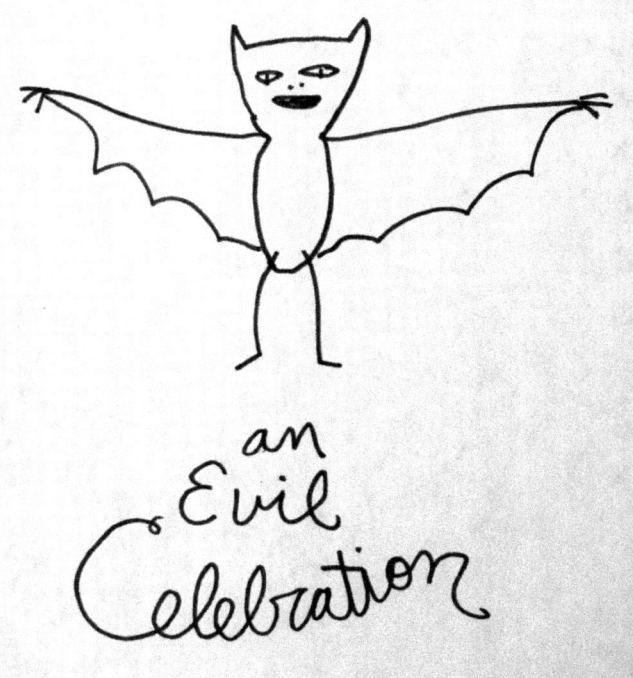

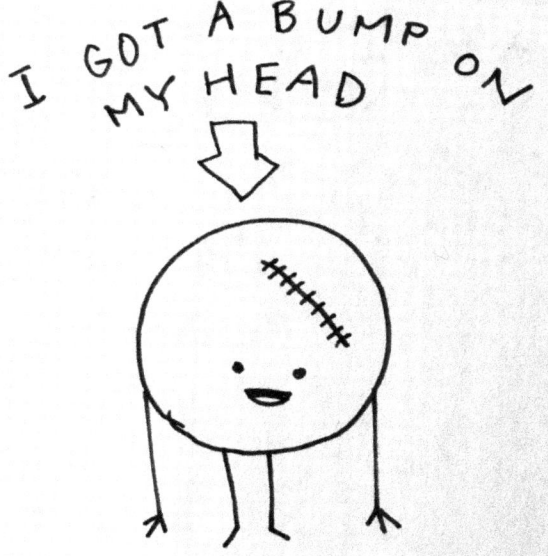

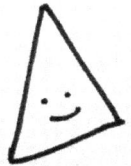

Here
we
go

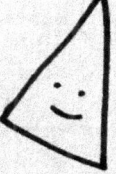

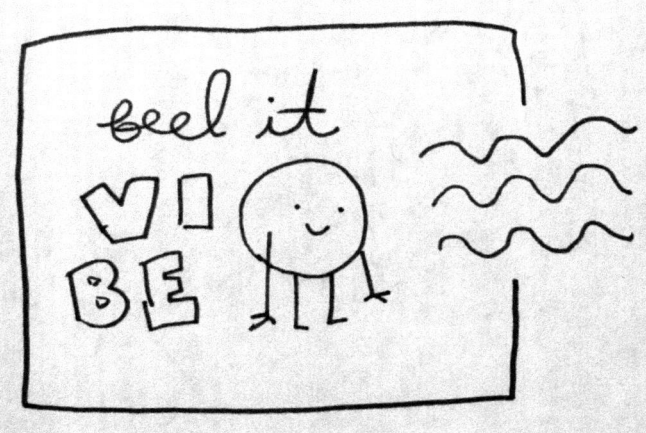

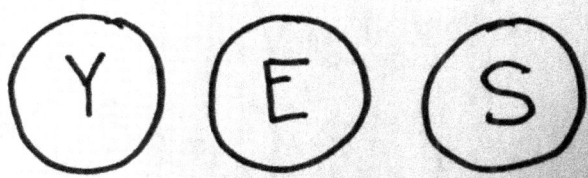

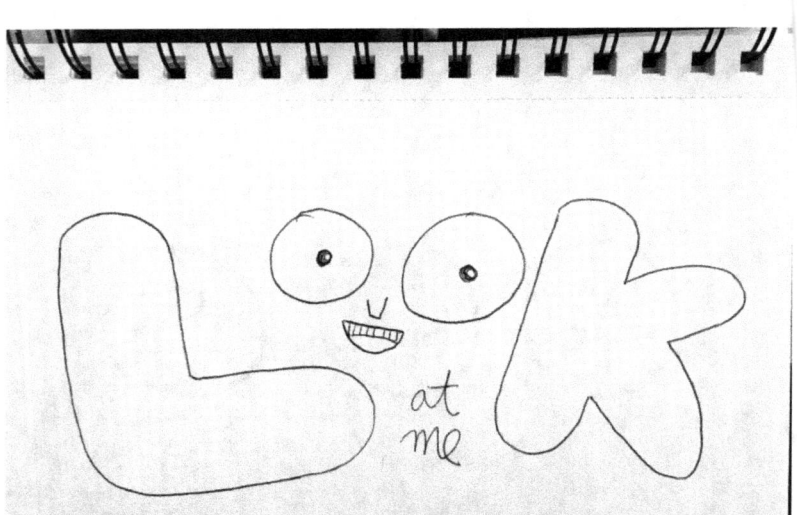

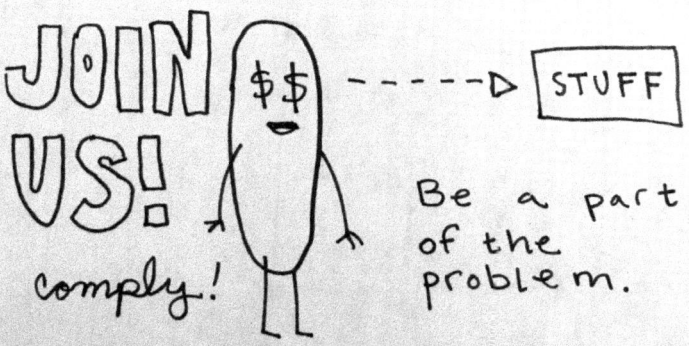

STAR FISH

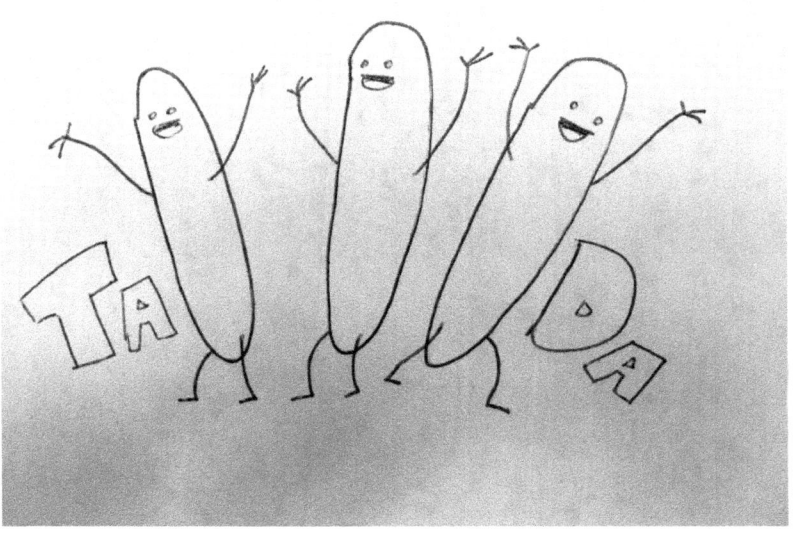

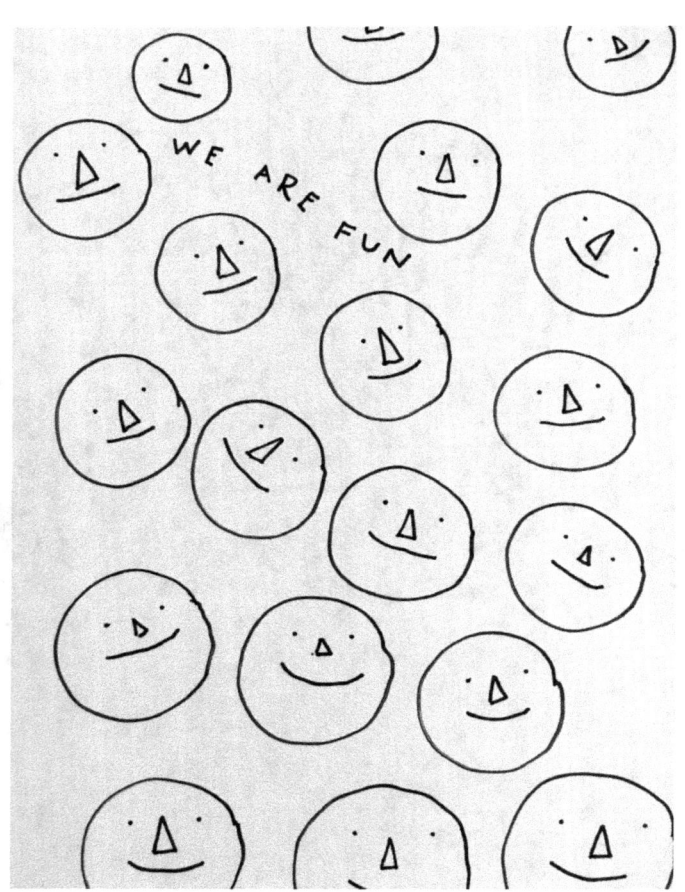

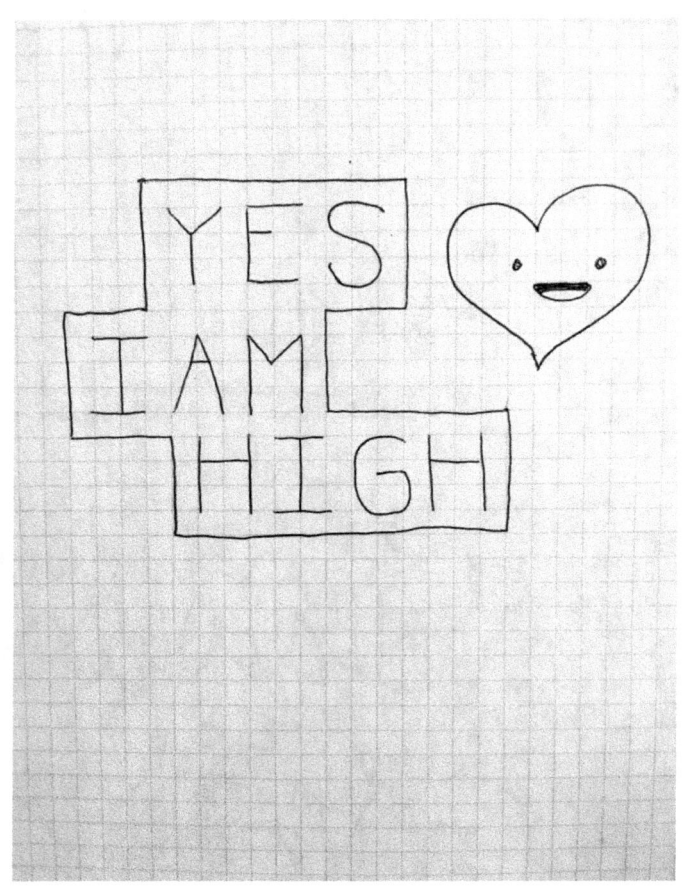

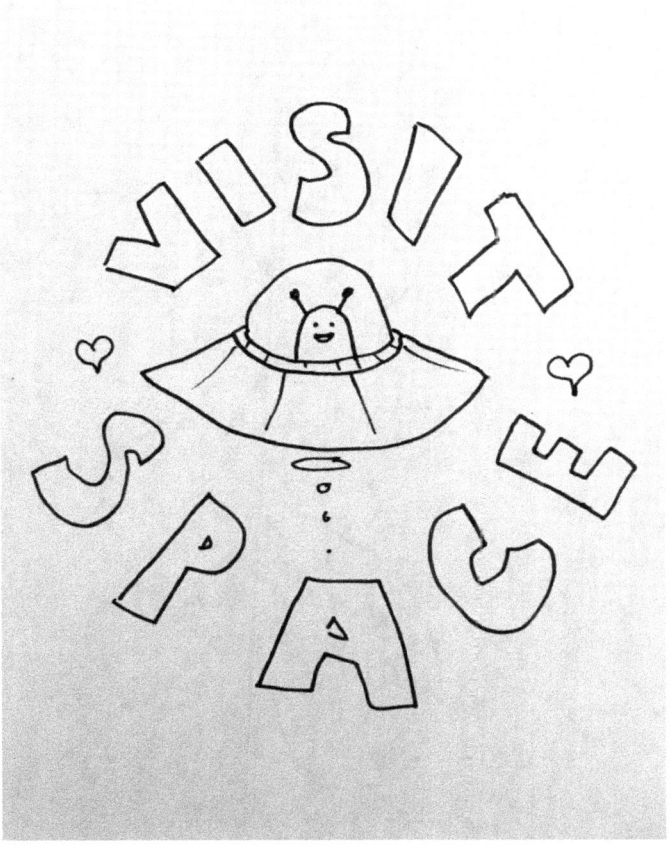

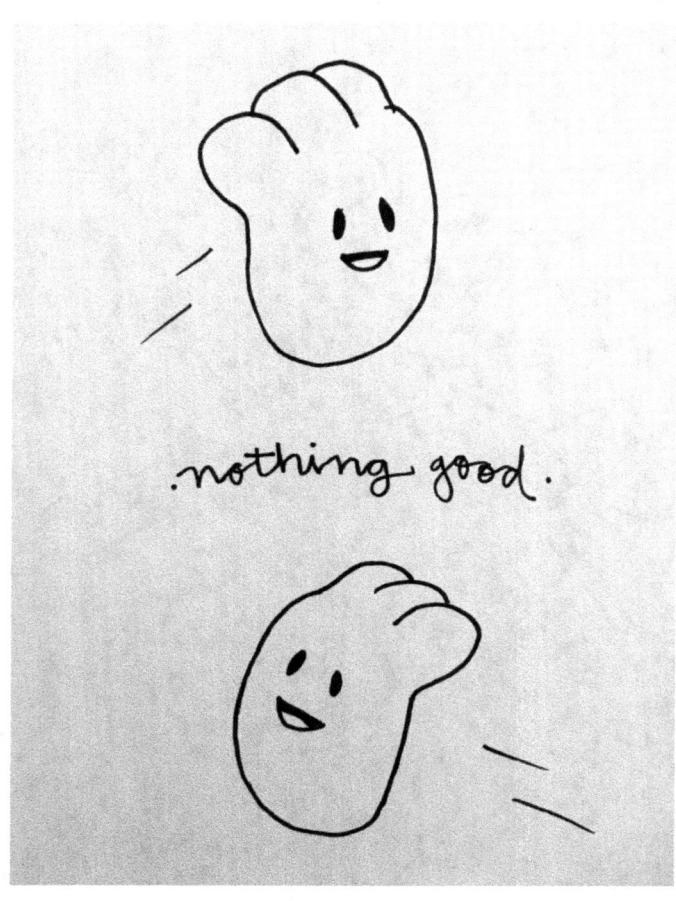

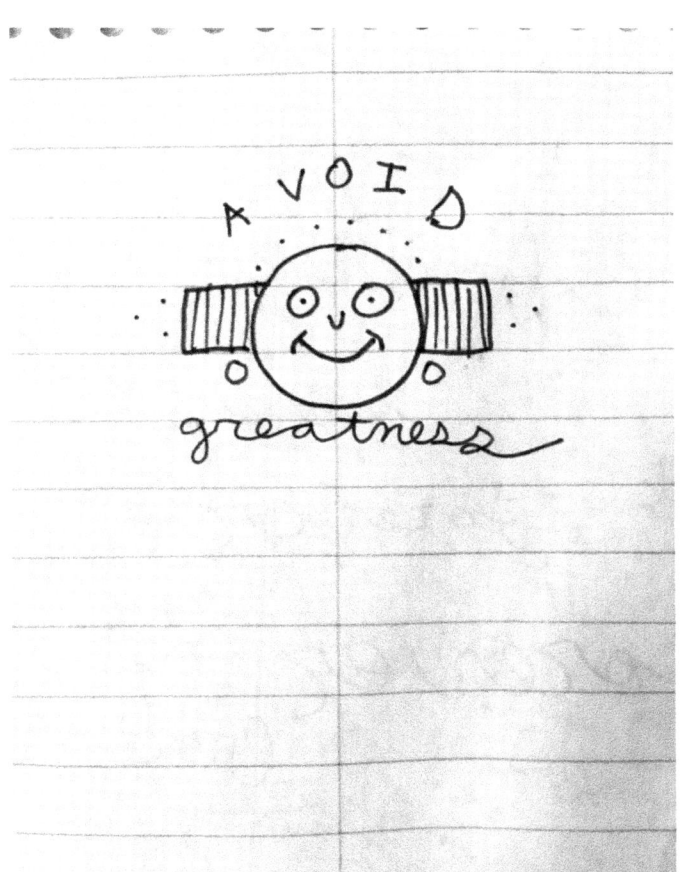

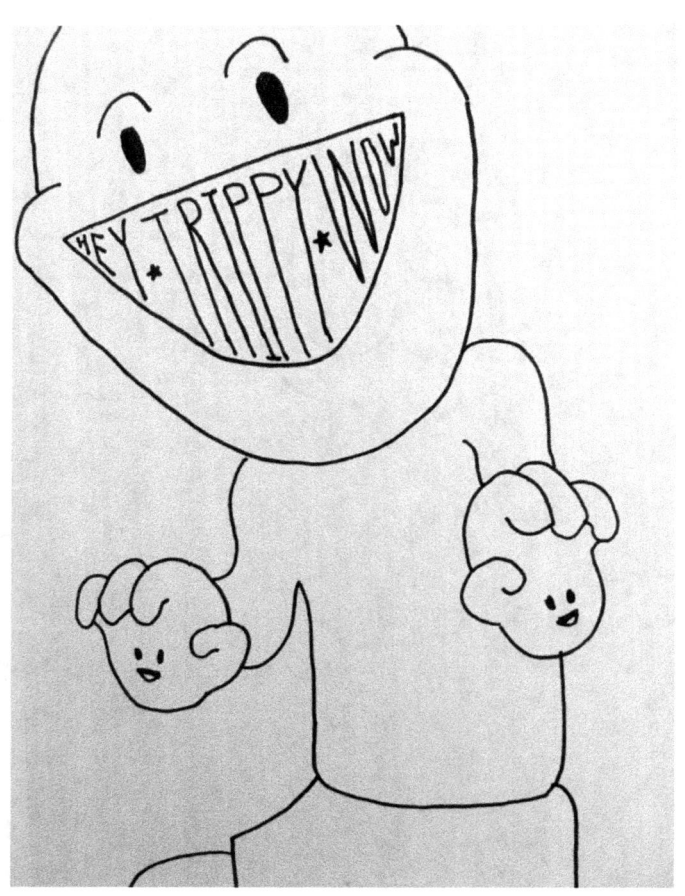

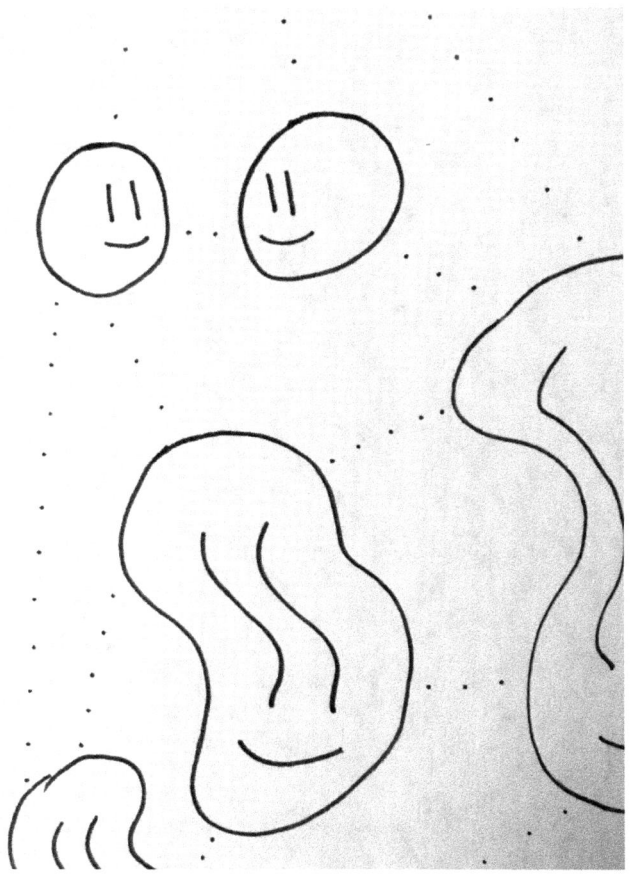

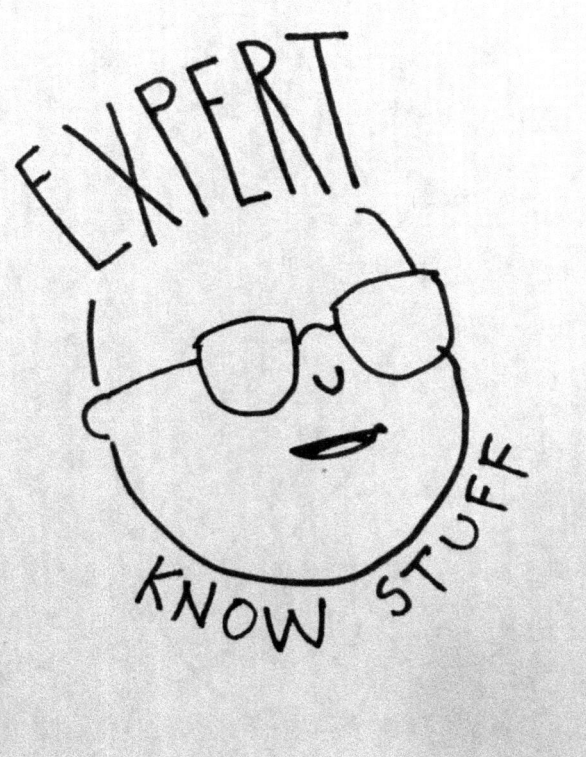

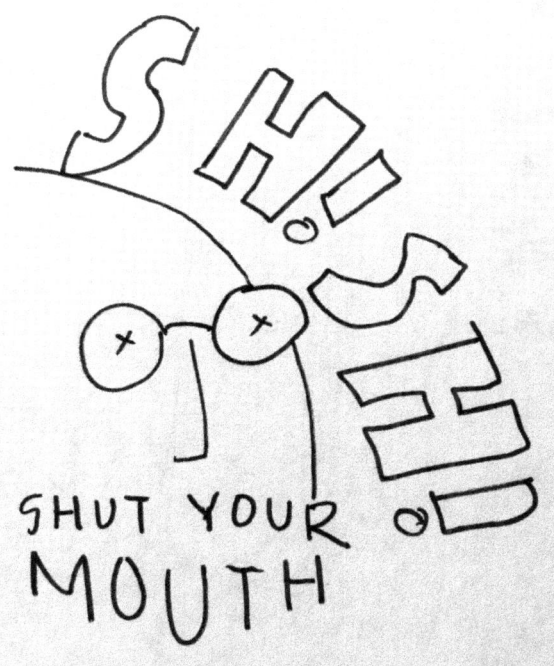

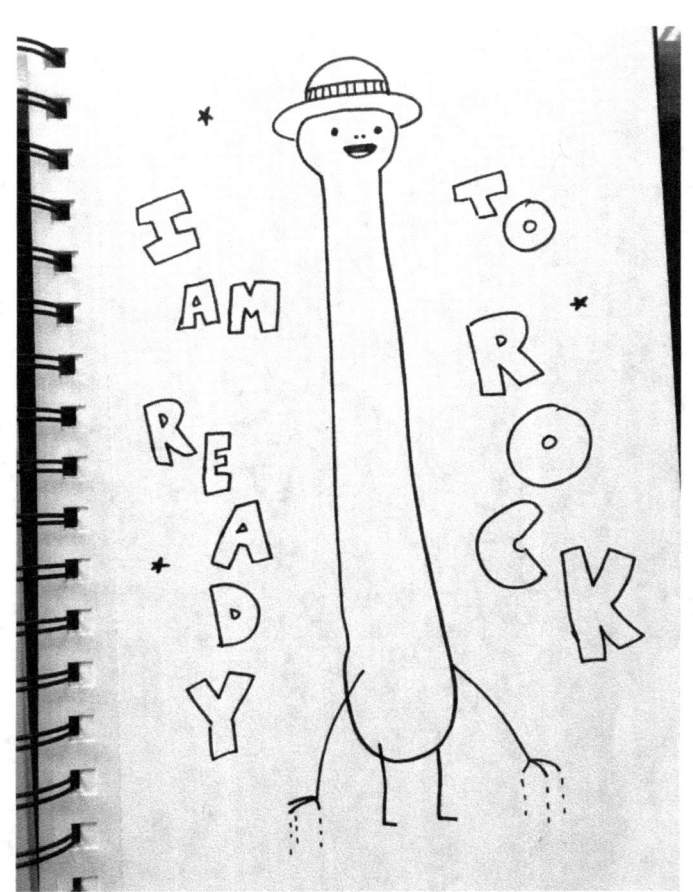

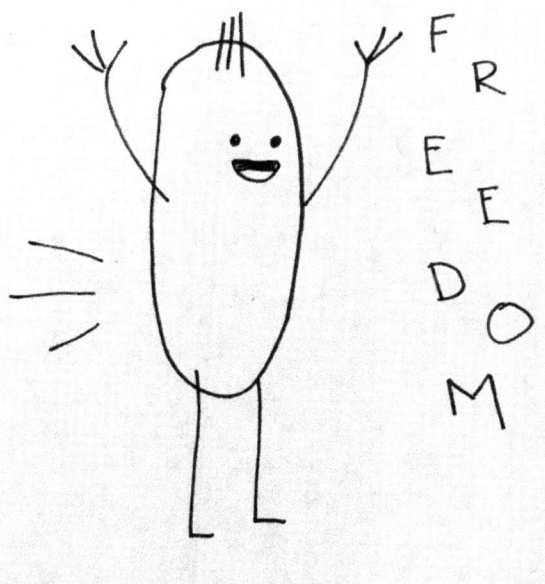

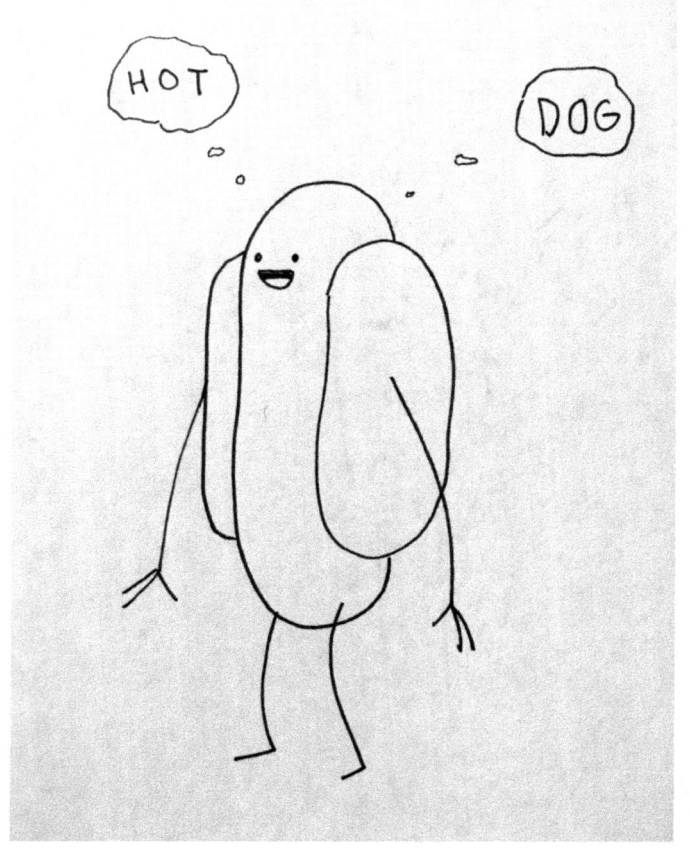

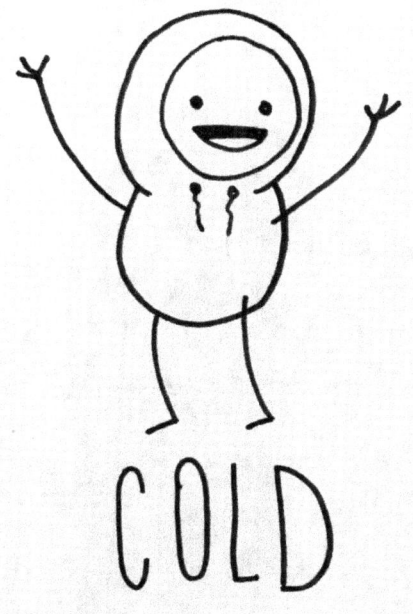

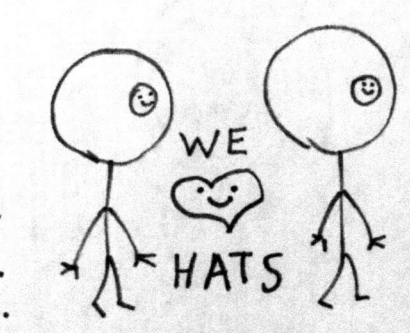

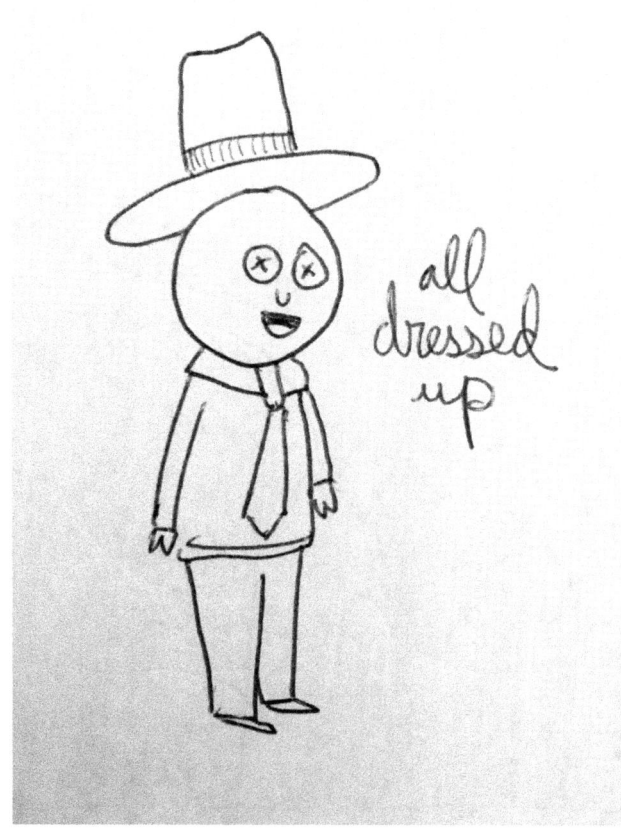

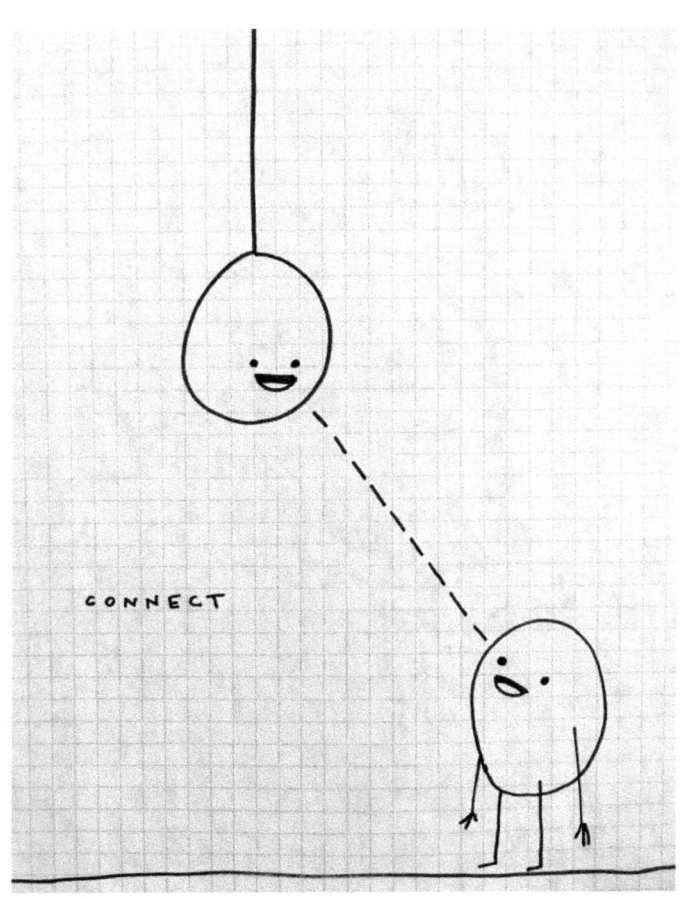

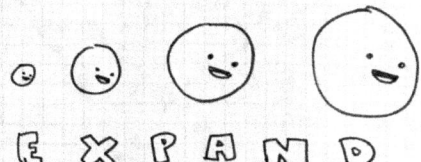

EXPAND

OR

DETACH

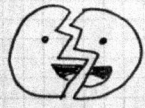

— — — — — — —

a choice for

YOU

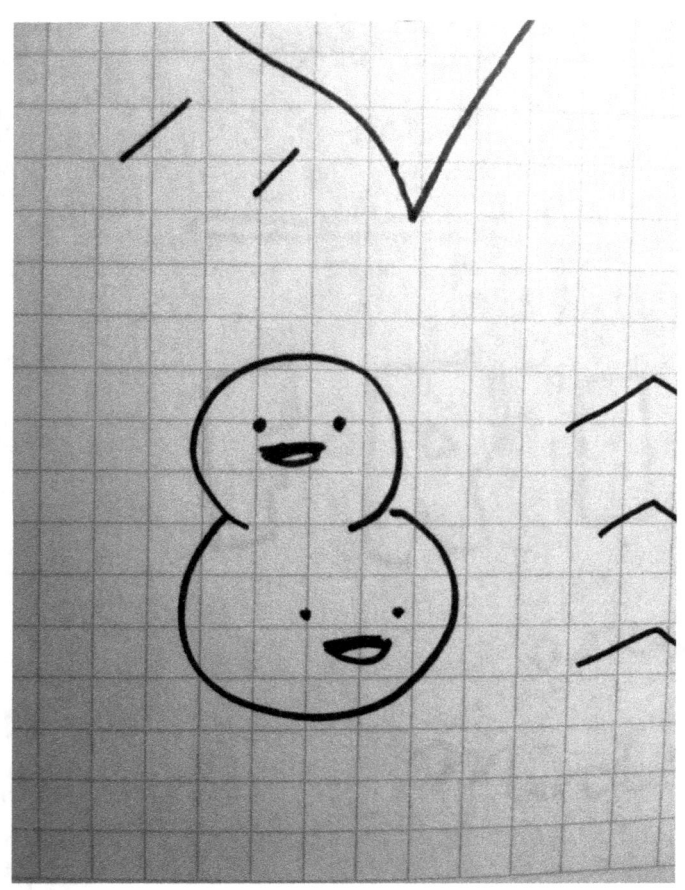

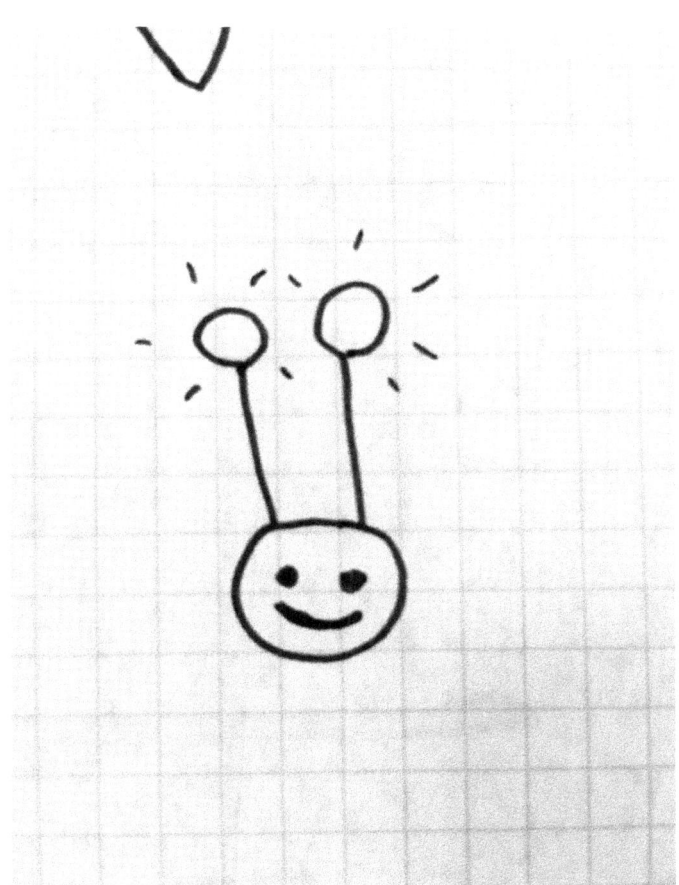

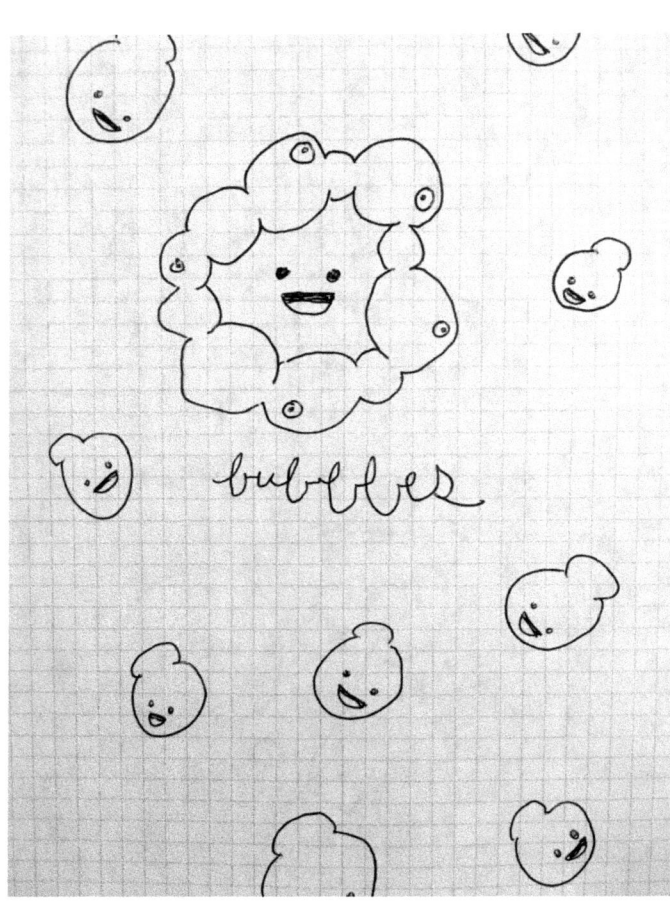

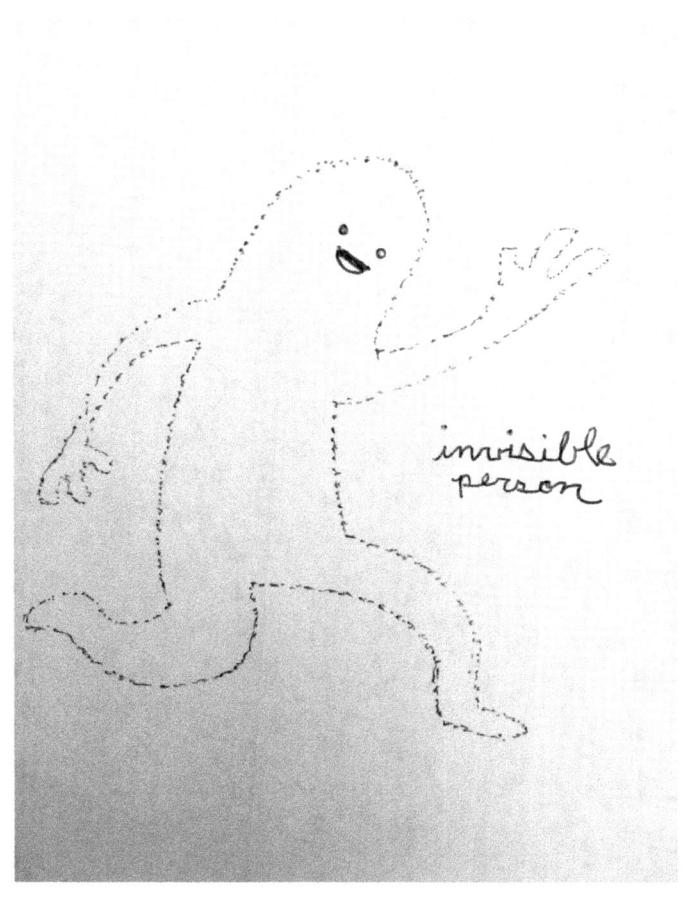

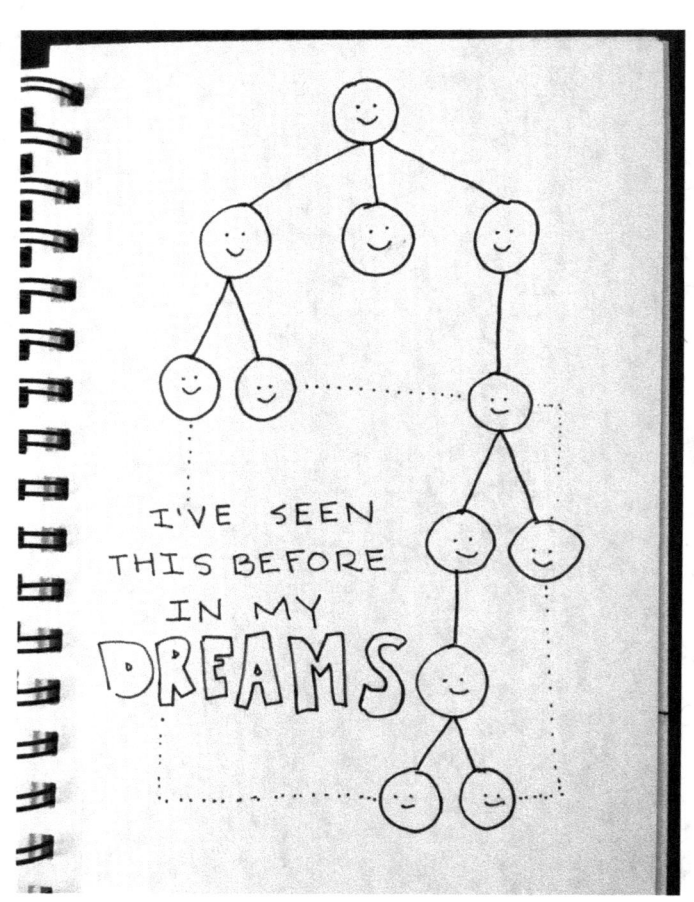

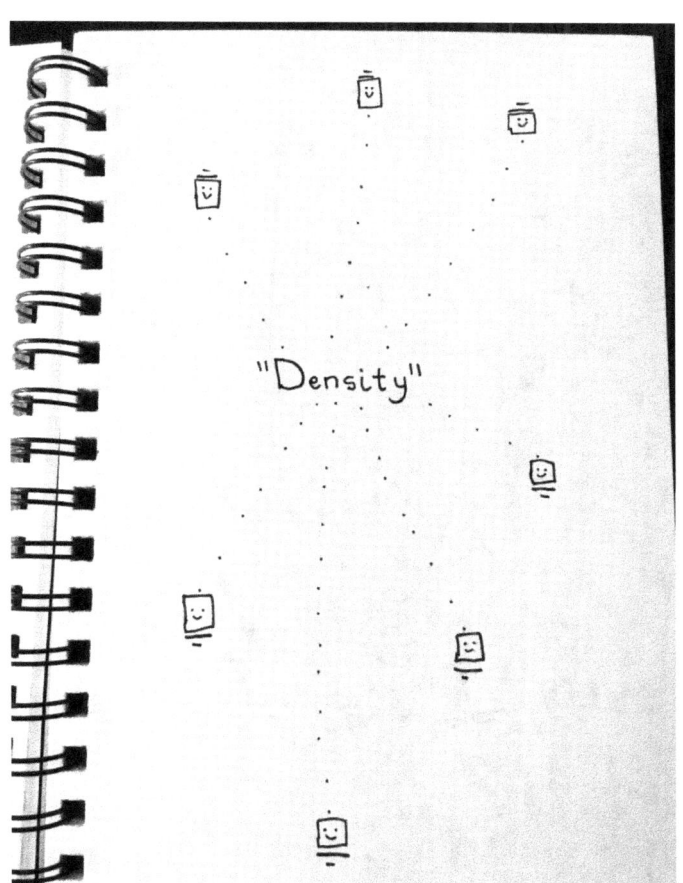

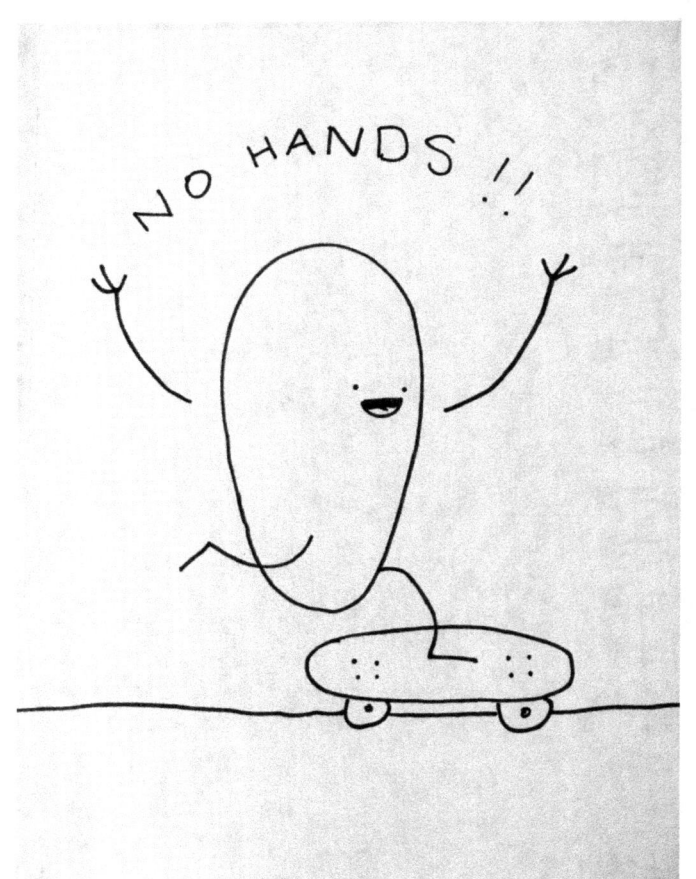

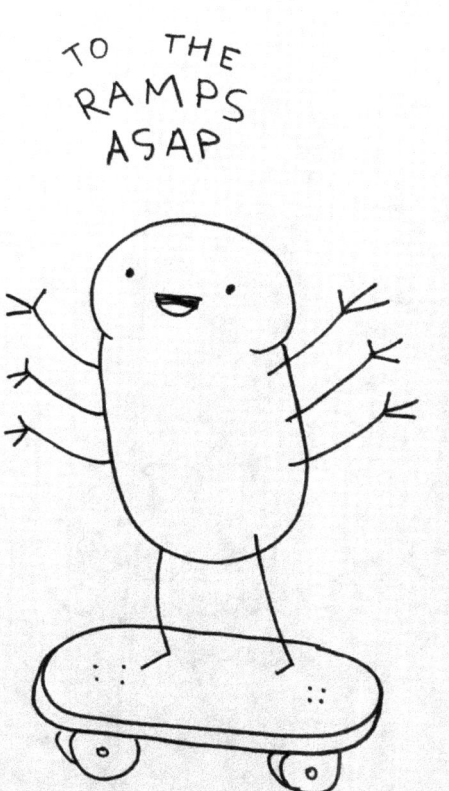

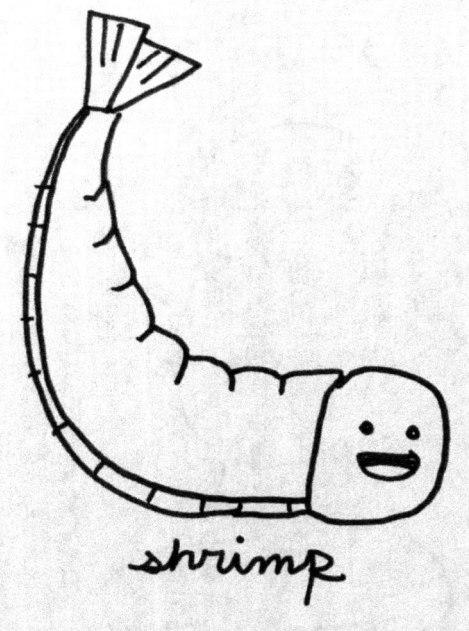

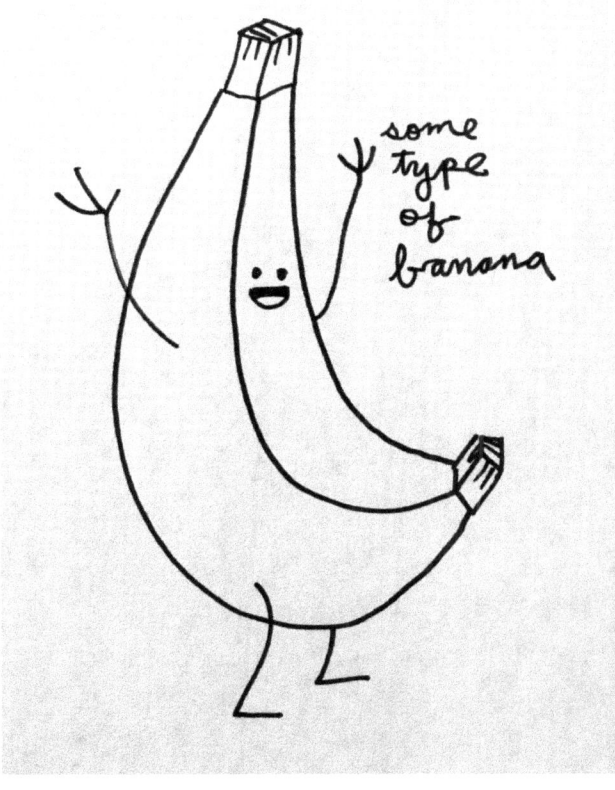

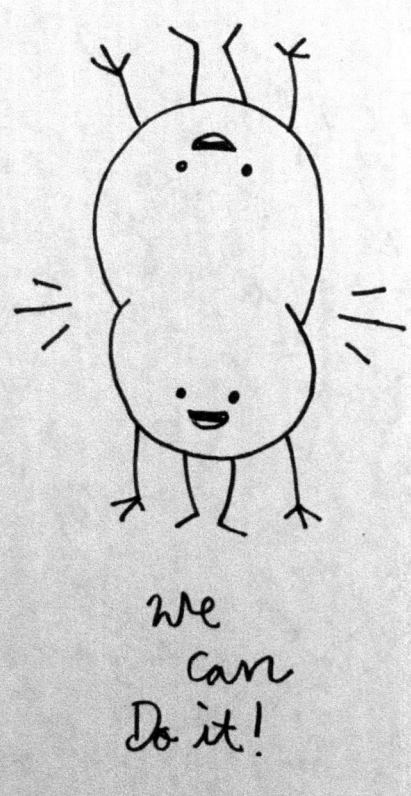

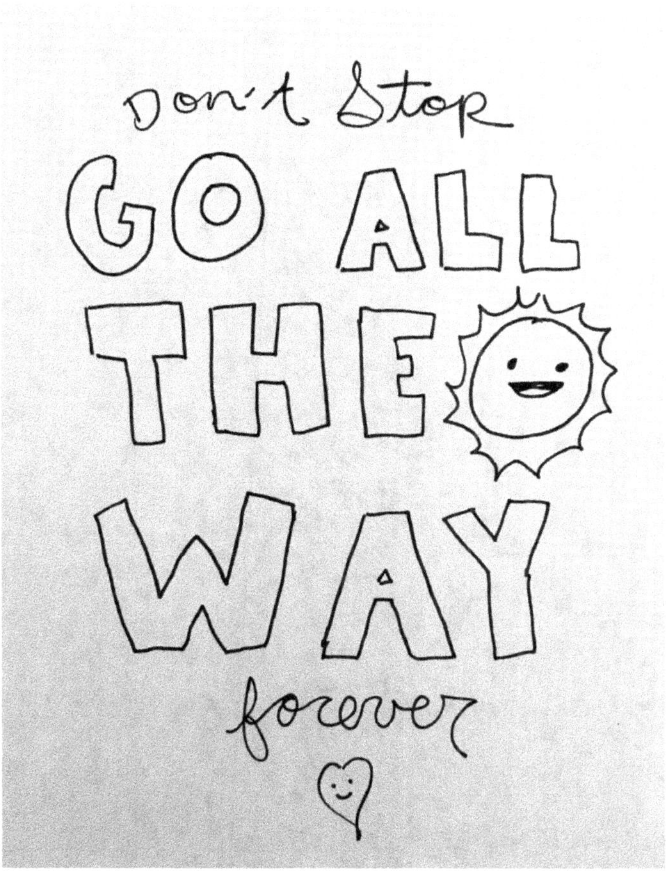

Don't Stop
GO ALL
THE
WAY
forever

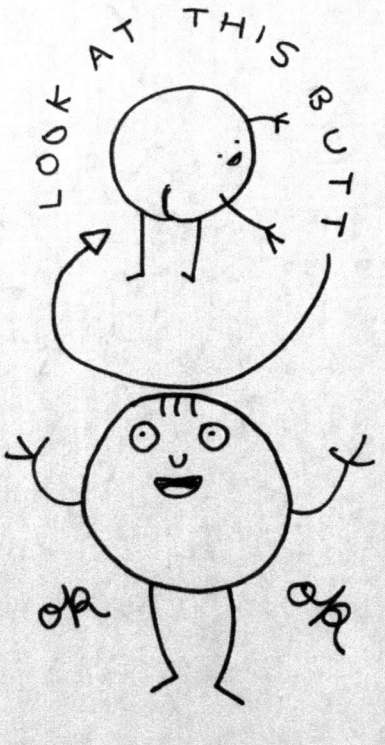

maybe!

YES!

NO!

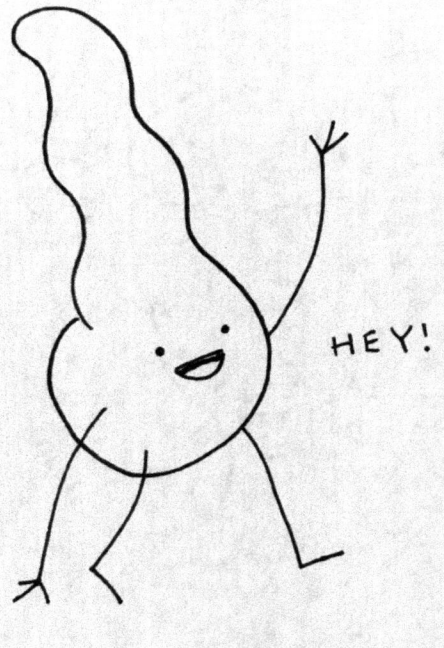

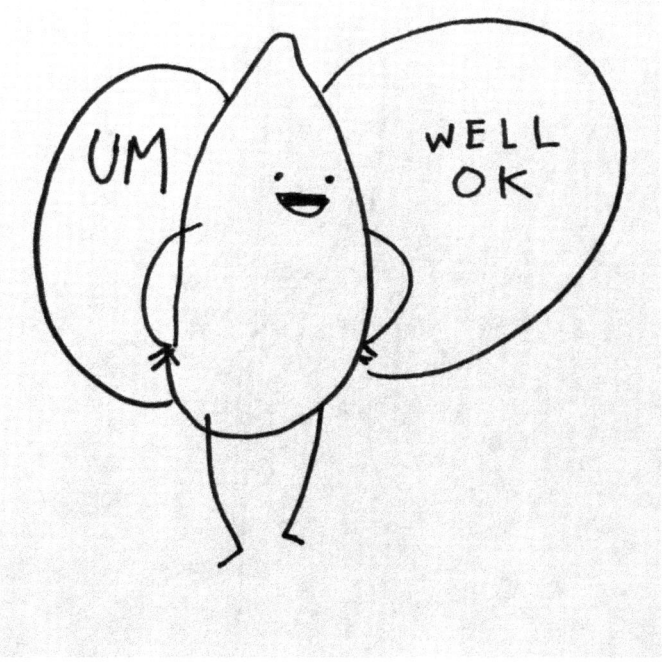

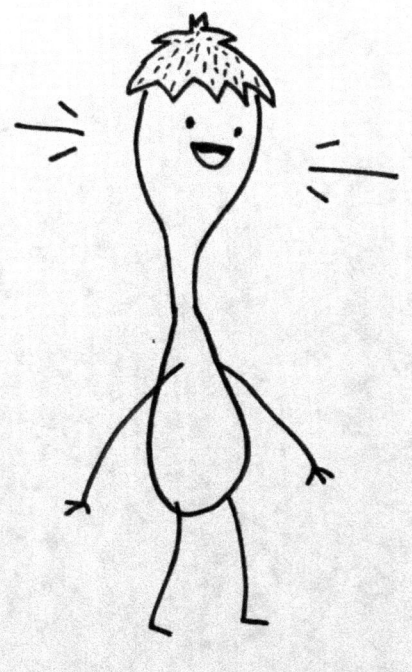

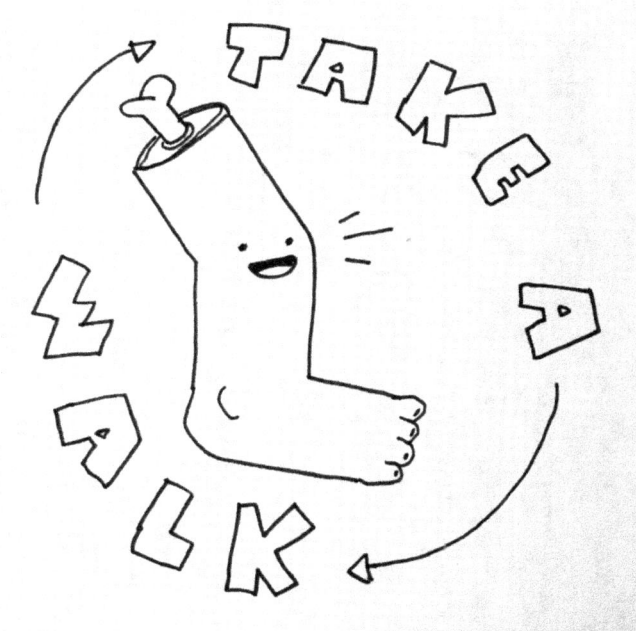

SMELLY

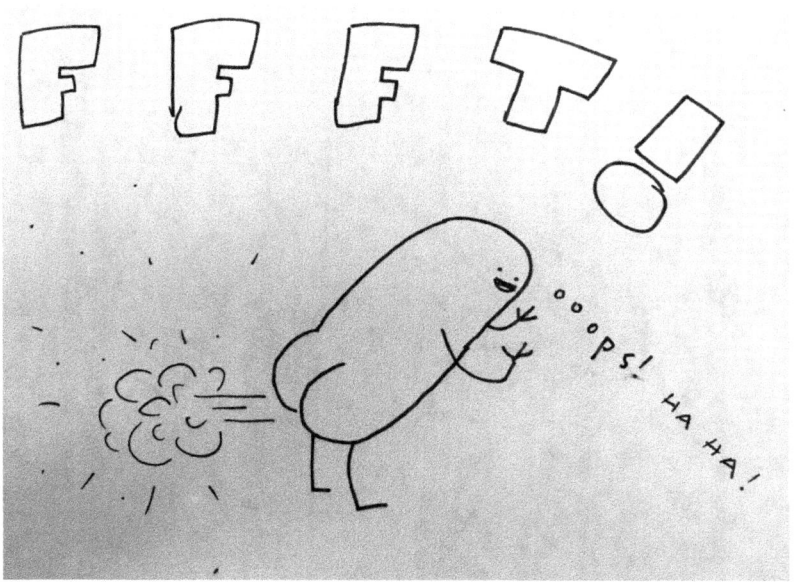

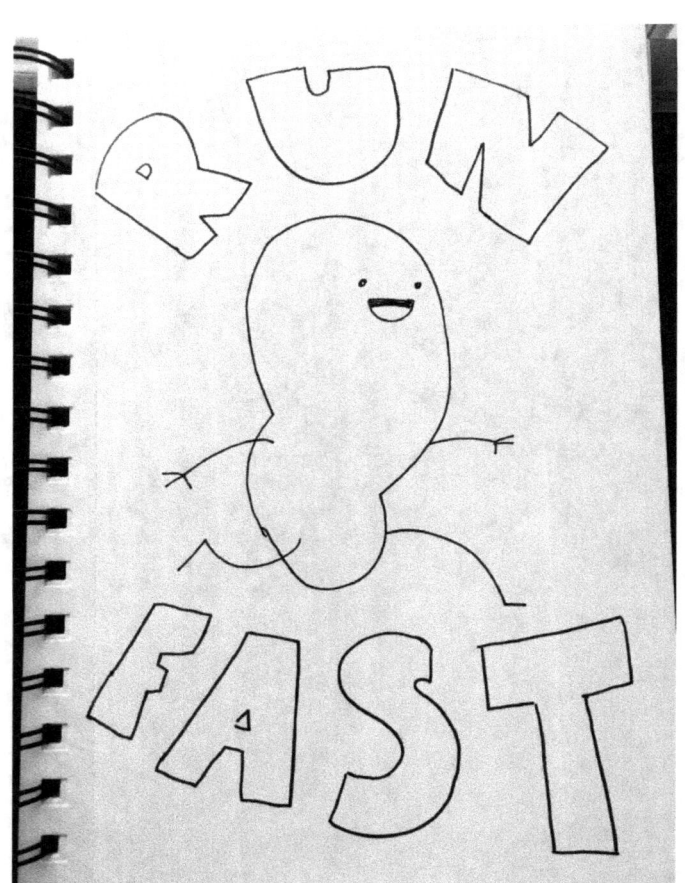

TO THE CLOUDS

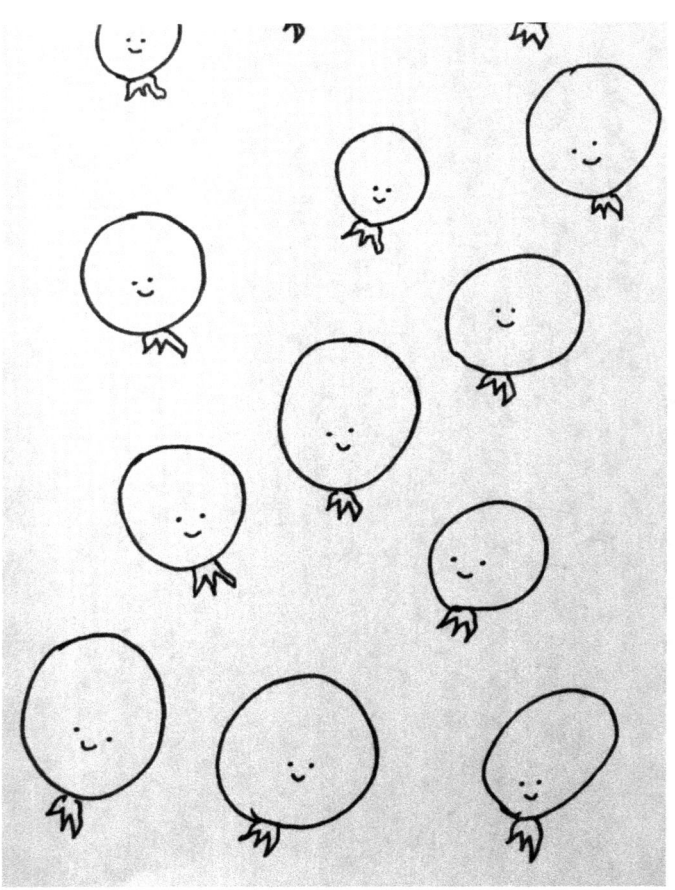

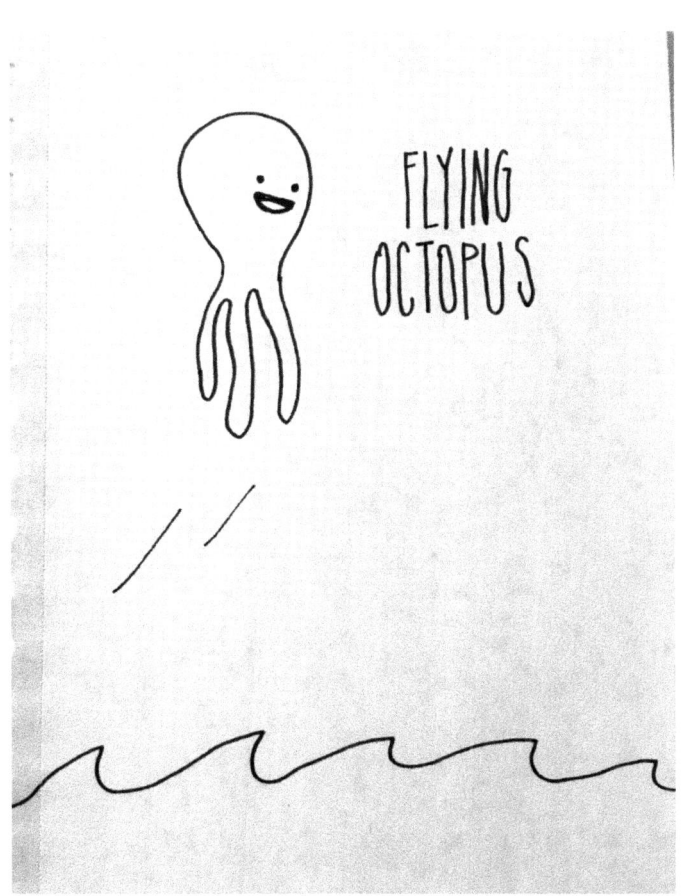

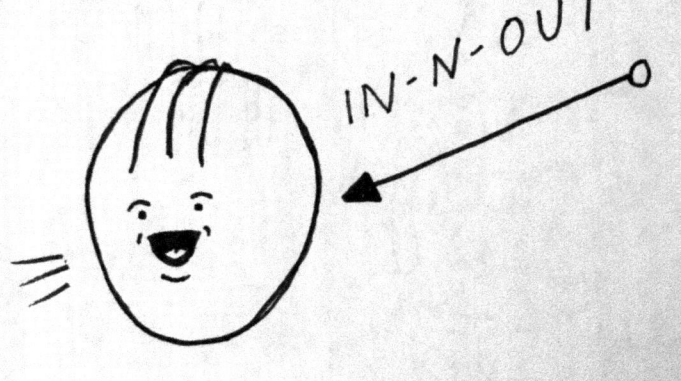

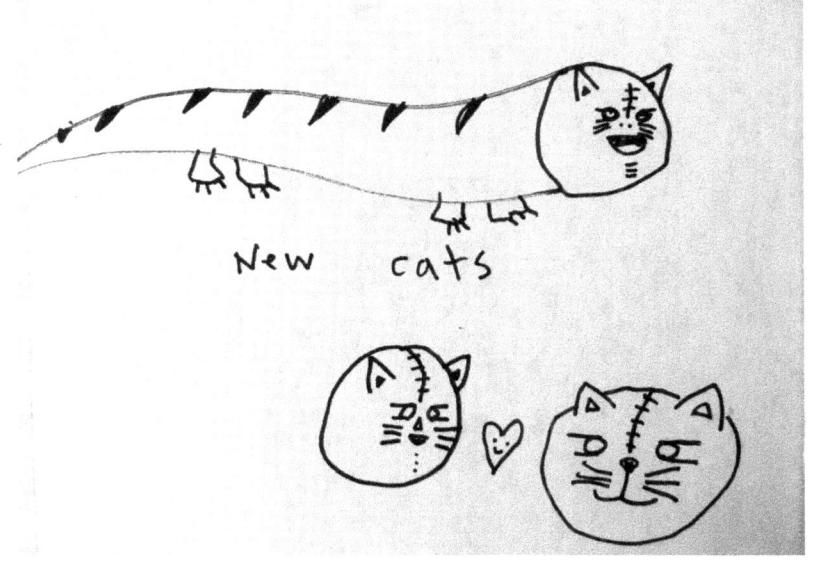

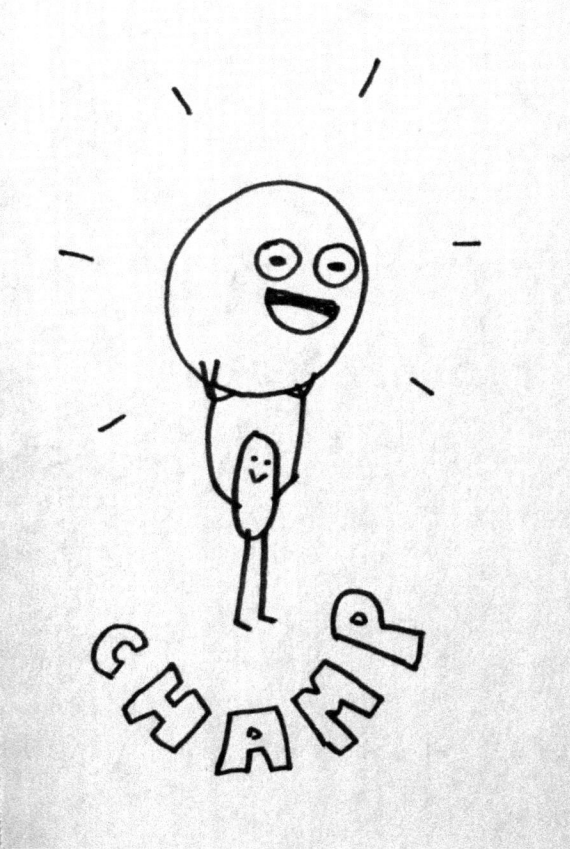

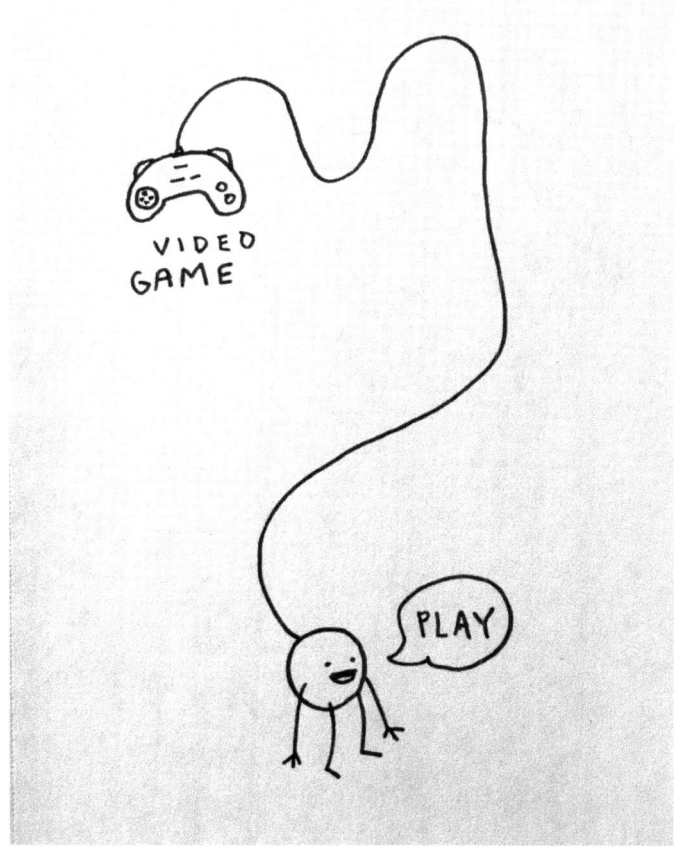

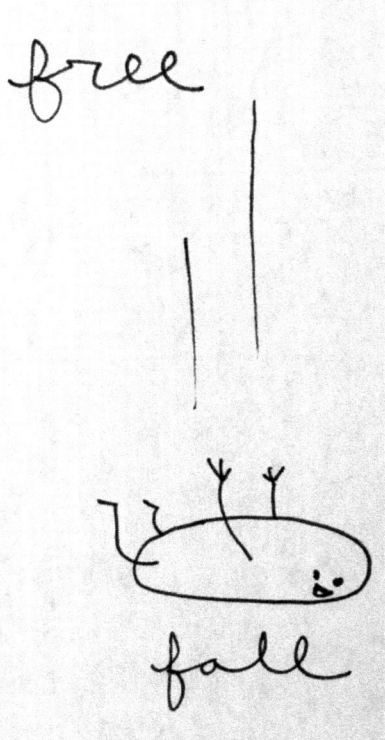

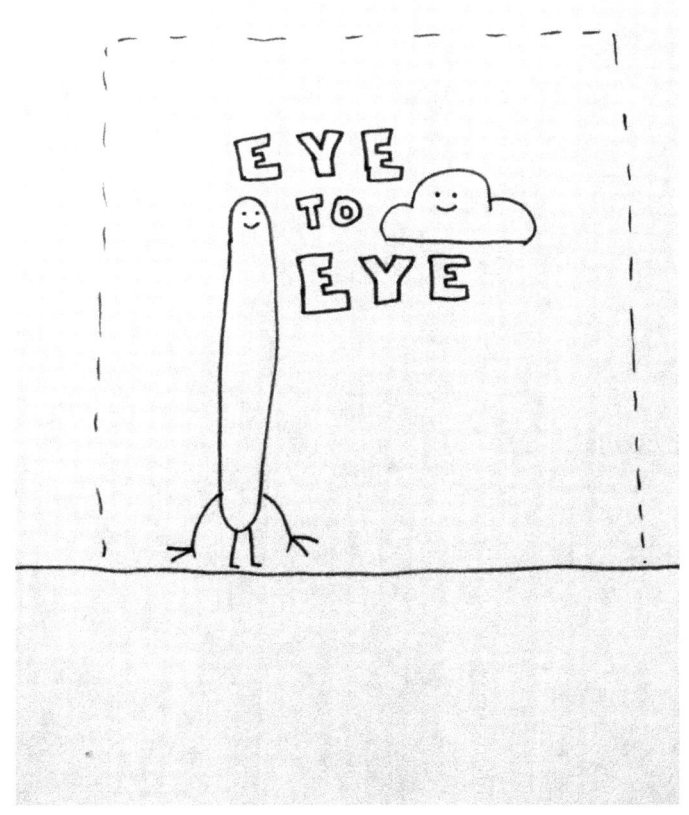

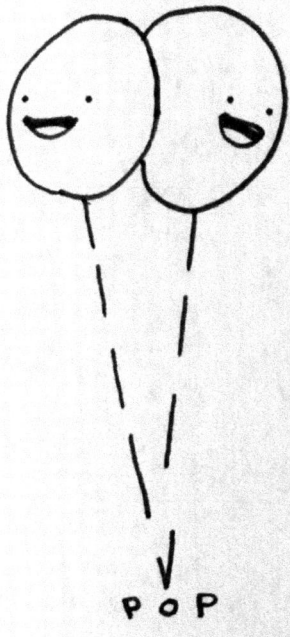

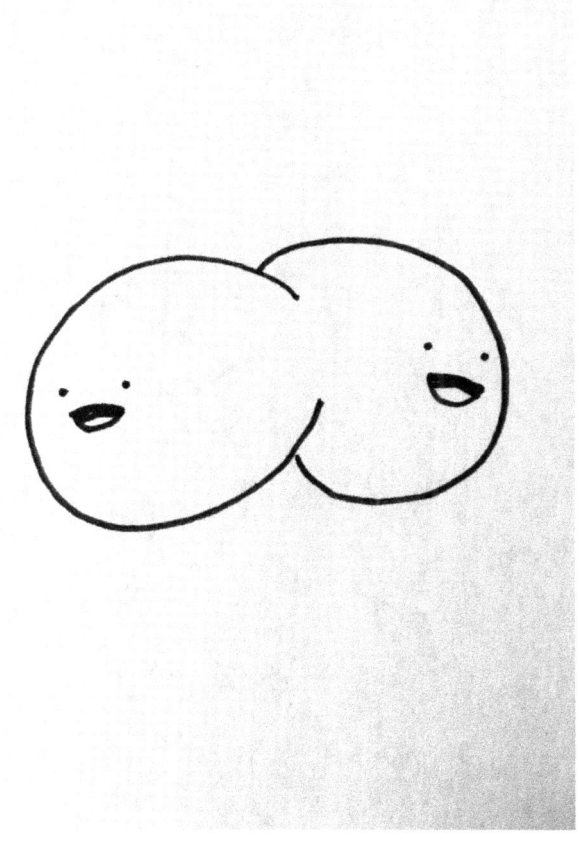

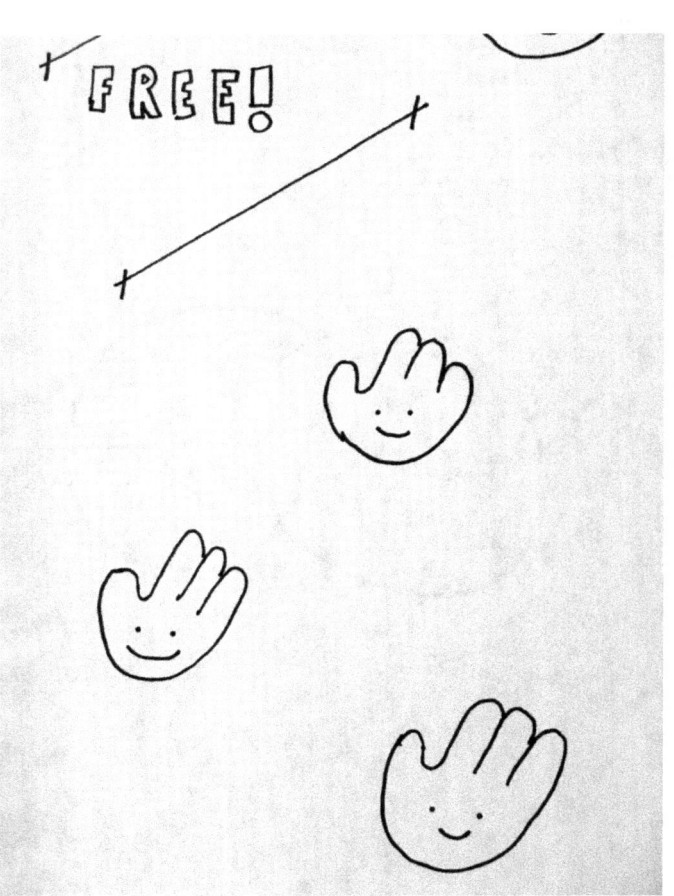

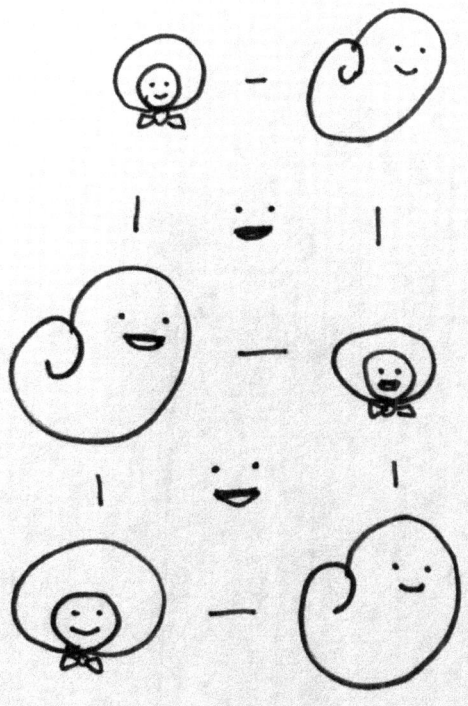

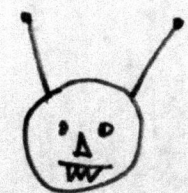

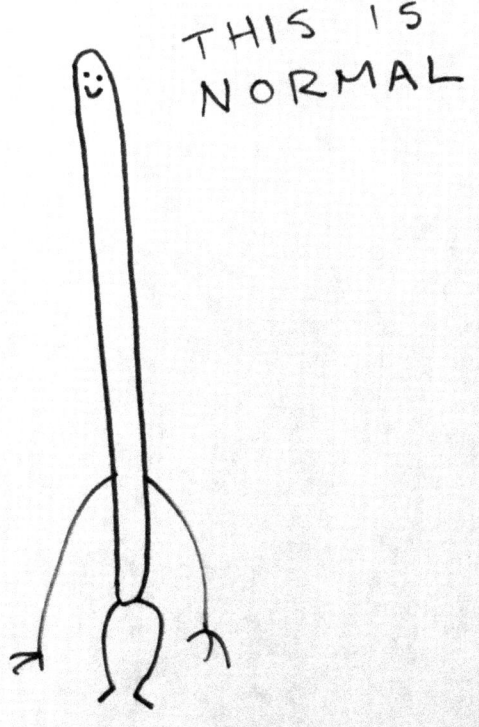

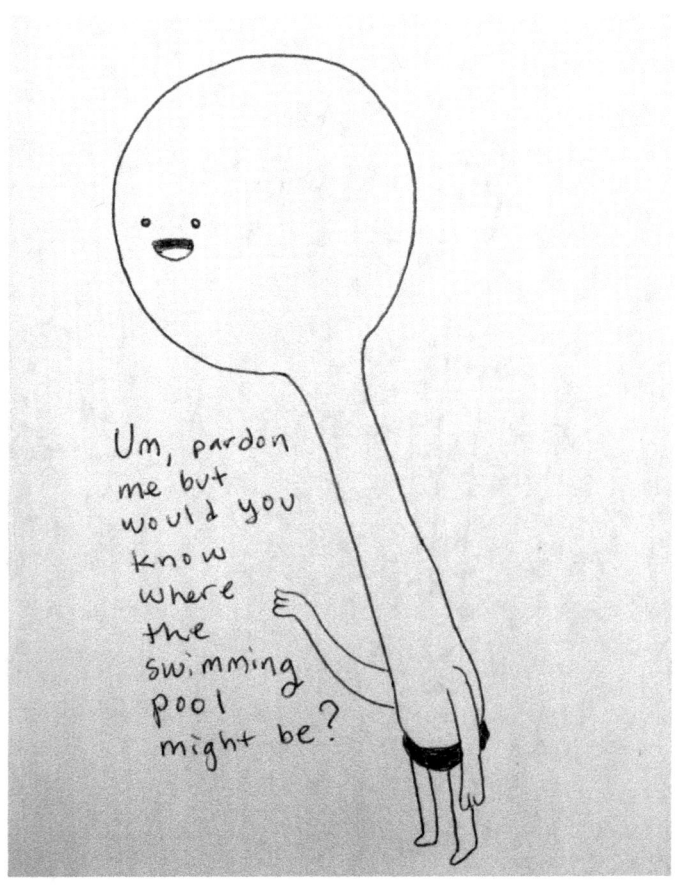

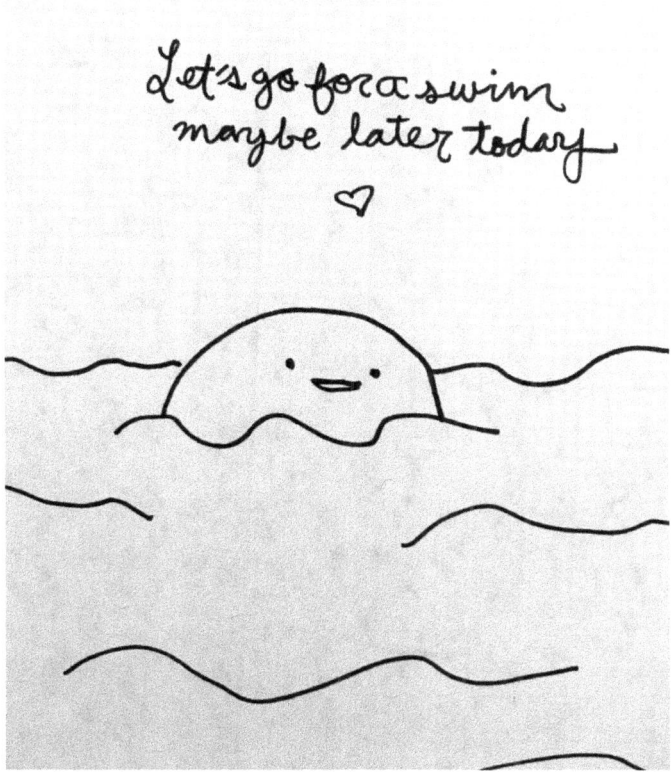

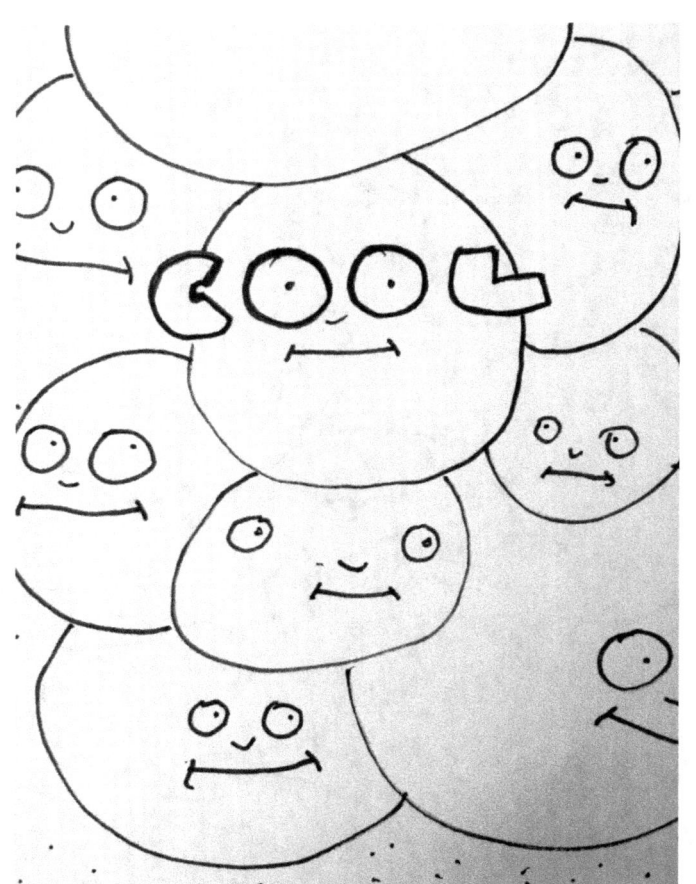

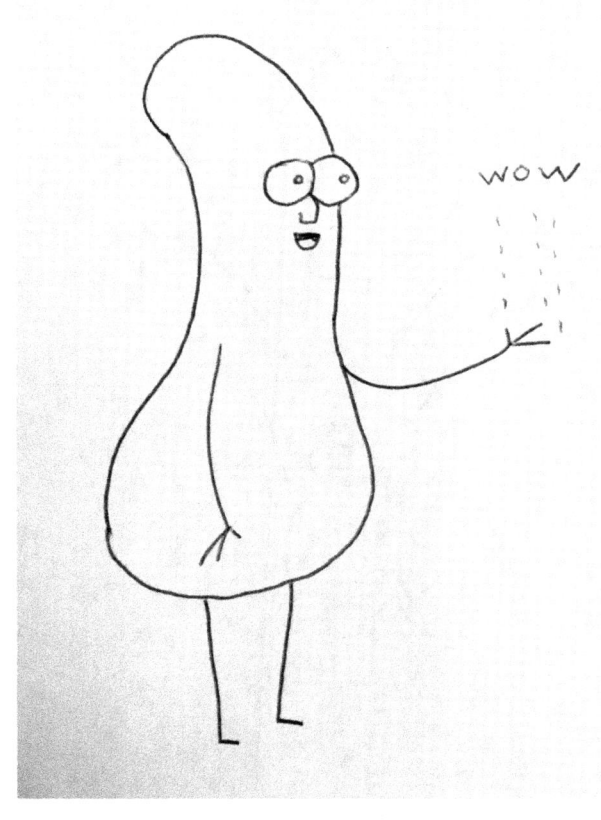

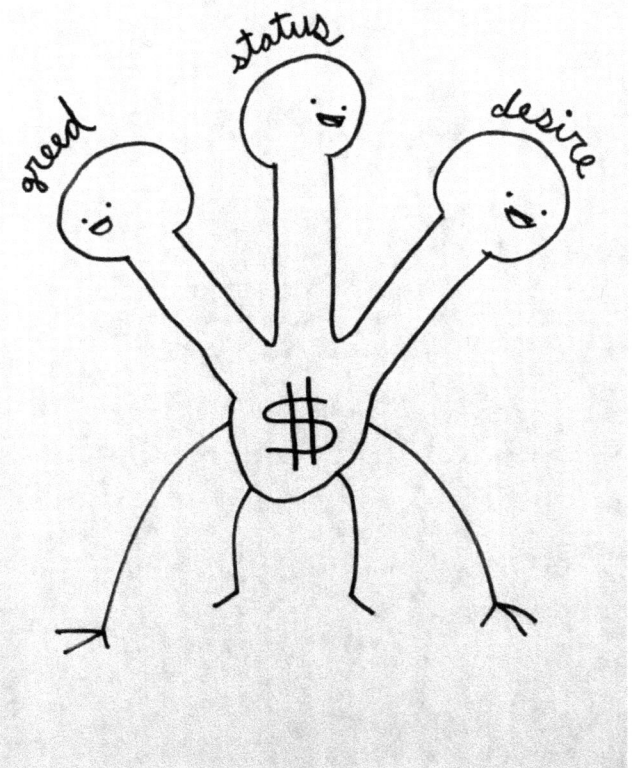

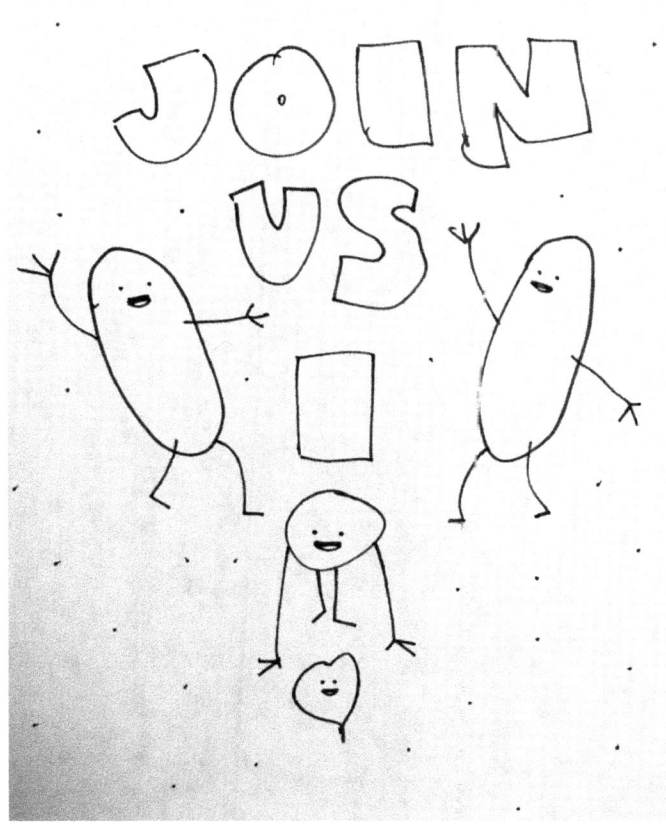

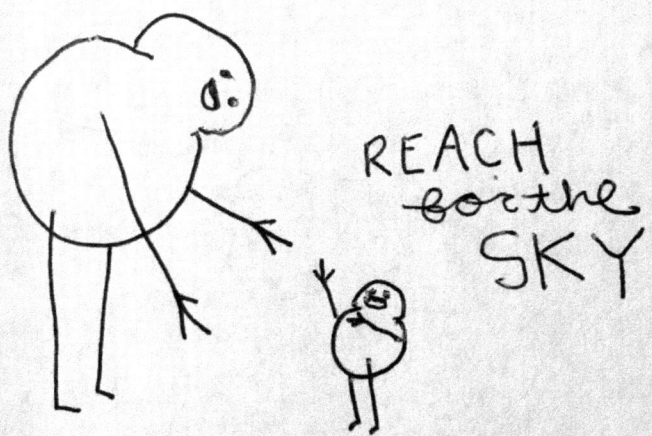

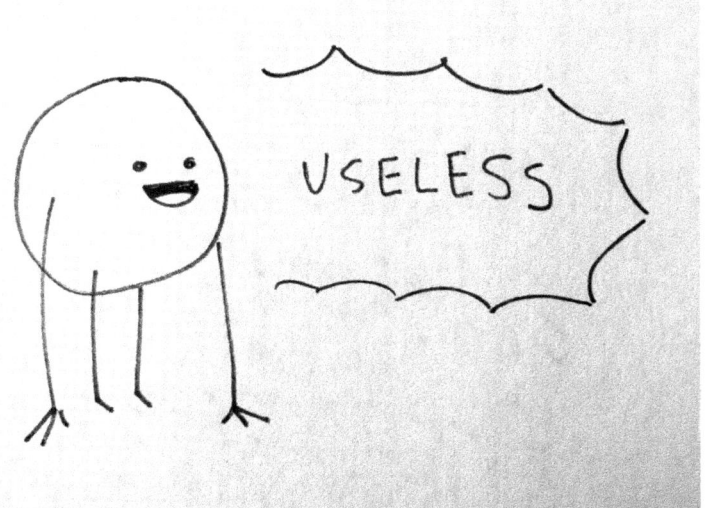

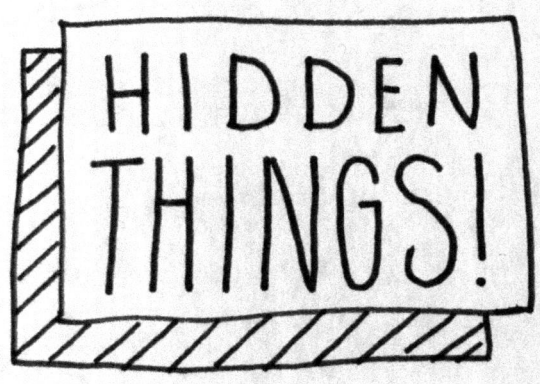

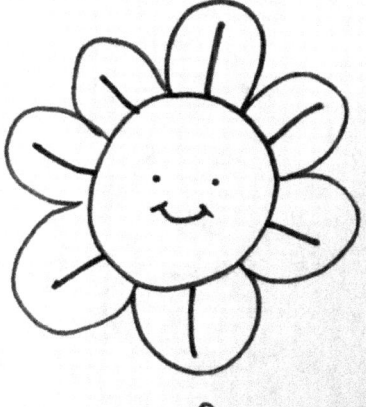

perfect

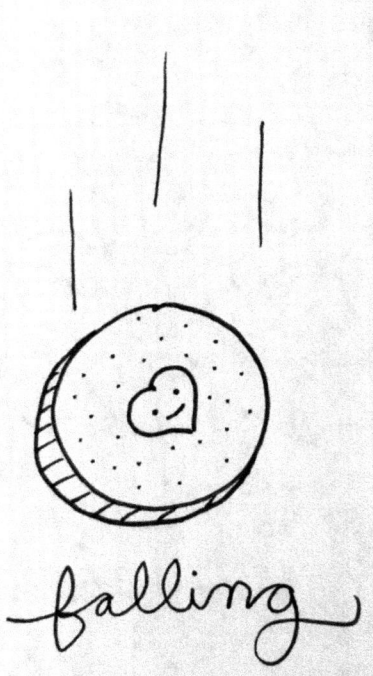

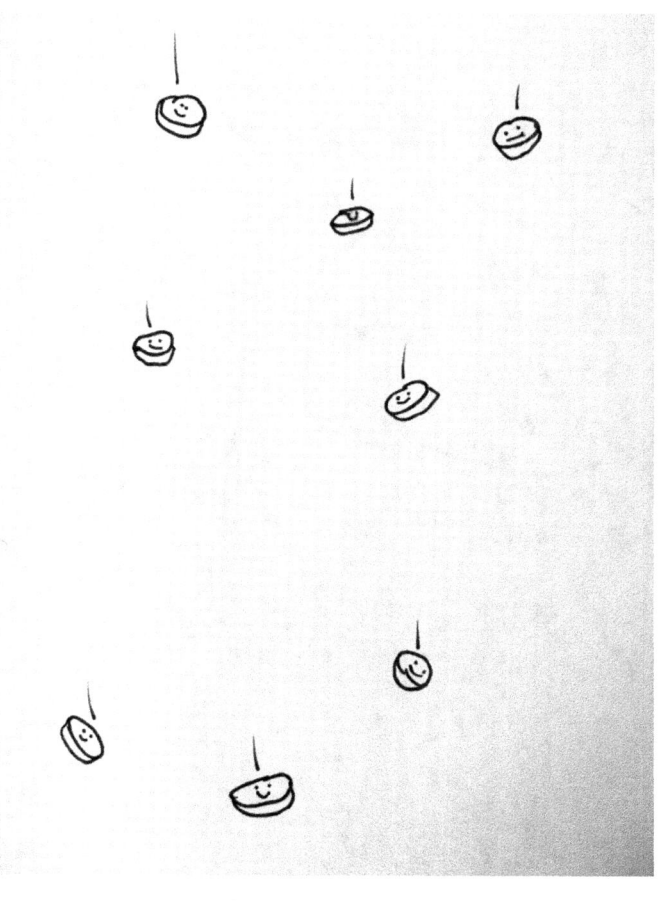

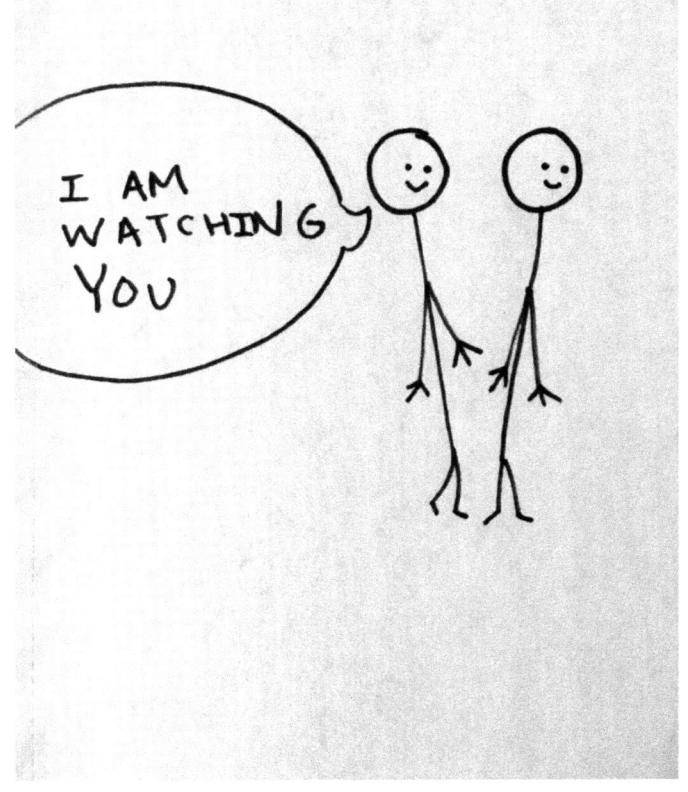

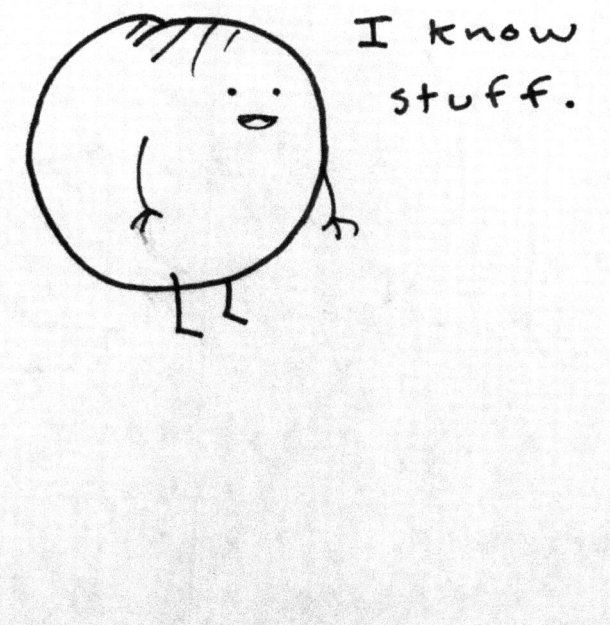

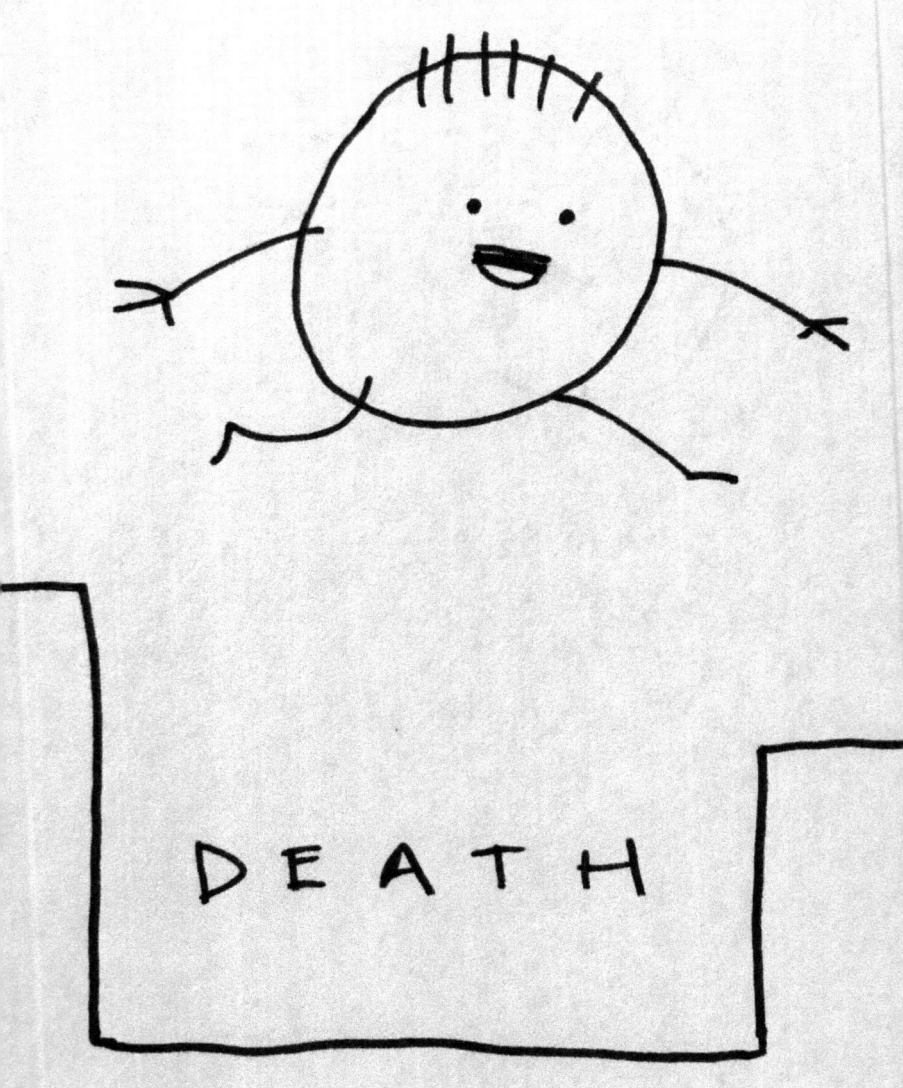

DOODLE

DOODLE

DOODLE

DOODLE

DOODLE

DOODLE

SKETCH

SKETCH

SKETCH

SKETCH

SKETCH

SKETCH

BOOKS
BOOKS
BOOKS
BOOKS
BOOKS
BOOKS

DRAW ~~DRIVE~~ FAST
DON'T STOP

PHOTOS & ILLUSTRATIONS BY
MATTHEW JOCELYN

www.ingramcontent.com/pod-product-compliance
Lightning Source LLC
Chambersburg PA
CBHW071422210526
45465CB00001B/495